STUDIES IN ROMANCE LANGUAGES: 34

John E. Keller, Editor

Aesop's Fables

With a Life of Aesop

Translated from the Spanish
with an Introduction by

John E. Keller and L. Clark Keating

THE UNIVERSITY PRESS OF KENTUCKY

Publication of this book was made possible by a grant
from The Program for Cultural Cooperation between
Spain's Ministry of Culture and
United States Universities.

Scholarly publisher for the Commonwealth,
serving Bellarmine College, Berea College, Centre
College of Kentucky, Eastern Kentucky University,
The Filson Club, Georgetown College, Kentucky
Historical Society, Kentucky State University,
Morehead State University, Murray State University,
Northern Kentucky University, Transylvania University,
University of Kentucky, University of Louisville,
and Western Kentucky University.

Editorial and Sales Offices: Lexington, Kentucky 40508-4008

Library of Congress Cataloging-in-Publication Data
Aesop's fables. English
    Aesop's fables, with a life of Aesop / Translated from the Spanish
with an introduction by John E. Keller and L. Clark Keating.
        p.   cm. — (Studies in Romance languages ; no. 34)
    Translated from the Spanish edition printed by Johan Hurus: La
vida del Ysopet con sus fabulas hystoriadas. Zaragoza?, 1489.
    Includes bibliographical references and index.
    ISBN 0-8131-1812-3
    1. Fables, Greek—Translations into English. I. Aesop.
II. Keller, John Esten. III. Keating, L. Clark (Louis Clark),
1907-. IV. Title. V. Series: Studies in Romance languages (Lexington,
Ky.) ; no. 34.
PQ6498.V2913   1993
398.24'52—dc20   92-2478

This book is printed on recycled acid-free paper meeting
the requirements of the American National Standard
for Permanence of Paper for Printed Library Materials.
∞

Contents

Contents

Contents

Contents

Contents

Contents

Contents

ESOPVS

Introduction

esop's Fables, with a Life of Aesop—in Spanish *La vida del Ysopet con sus fabulas hystoriadas*—along with versions with similar titles in many western languages, represents the apogee of that body of stories we know as Aesop's Fables. This may seem an unusual statement to make, since the *Ysopet,* as we shall term it in this introduction, was not translated into Castilian until the late fifteenth century and not printed in its entirety in Spain until 1489. An incomplete version was printed in Saragossa in 1482 with woodcuts colored by hand. According to Victoria Burrus, who pointed out to me the existence of this incomplete incunable, the 1489 edition we have used as the basis of our translation is a corrected and augmented version of the 1482 text. While the 1482 edition should be the basis of a critical edition, since it is incomplete it cannot be the text from which a translation should be made. The edition of 1488, printed in Toulouse and edited by Victoria Burrus and Harriet Goldberg, would not have influenced the many Spanish versions listed by Cotarelo y Mori in his introduction to the facsimile edition of *Ysopete hystoriado* of 1489. The edition of 1482 would quite probably have been the one used by the printer in Toulouse. Be that as it may, since the text of 1482 is incomplete, and since the text of Toulouse of 1488 contains woodcuts not as excellent as those in the printing of 1489 in Saragossa, we are confident that our choice of edition is best for the present translation, which is the first into the English language.

To begin with, we do not know if indeed in the sixth century B.C. there actually lived an author named Aesop any more than we can be certain that about three thousand years ago a man named Homer flourished. But we believe in an Aesop because ancient writers of consequence—Herodotus, Plato, and Aristotle, to name but three—mention him as a fabulist and because various ancient writers—Babrius, Phaedrus, Avianus, and others—gathered and set down fables they attributed to him. No manuscripts of Aesop have survived from that early period and, what is worse, nothing like a complete collection of those fables has survived the ages. We do not know, therefore, how many fables go back to the original collections. But fables attributed to Aesop were gathered and set down in writing across the centuries, some collections copious and some limited as to number, in both Greek and Latin. Wherever Greek colonists went in ancient times, they surely took some of the fables with them, and in Spain this would have scattered Aesop along the eastern seaboard. Roman conquerors and settlers surely brought Aesop with them to Rome's favorite colony.

Closer to us, because Aesop began to appear in the vernacular literatures of the West, is the impact of Aesop in the Middle Ages. In Spain, Odo of Cheriton's *Fabulae,* containing a great deal of Aesopic material, was probably translated from the Latin in the thirteenth century, when Odo flourished, even though the only extant manuscript of it in Spanish translation, *El libro de los gatos,* is of fifteenth-century vintage. The collection of eastern fables and stories *Kalila wa Dimna,* translated from the Arabic in 1251 at the behest of Prince Alfonso (to be crowned in 1252 as Alfonso X) and entitled *Calila e Digna,* contained some Aesopic fables, attesting to the fact that Aesop had penetrated the literatures of the Islamic world. In the fourteenth century Juan Ruiz, Archpriest of Hita, inserted more than twenty-five Aesopic fables into his *Libro de buen amor,* and his contemporary Don Juan Manuel adapted several in his *Conde Lucanor.* In the first quarter of the fifteenth century the Archdeacon Clemente Sánchez used a considerable number in his *Libro de los exenplos por a.b.c.,* the most copious book of brief narratives in the medieval Spanish language. Aesop, then, was well known in Spain long before the printing of the *Ysopet.*

We must trace the ancestry of Spain's great corpus of Aesopic fables as they appeared in the West to the Middle Ages' most comprehensive anthology collected and written down in one volume in medieval Greek by Maximus Planudius, ambassador to Venice from Constantinople in 1327. From what sources this ecclesiastic garnered the many fables he set down is not known, nor do we know the authorship of the fictitious thirteenth-century *Life of Aesop* which Planudius included as an important preface to his anthology of fables. It is certain that he did not stop with fables considered as belonging to an Aesopic tradition, for he included a good many brief narratives definitely not fables at all. These stemmed from eastern tales, many of which originated in the *Panchatantra,* written in Sanskrit, and passed through Pahlevi into Arabic and thence into Planudius's native Greek. It is even possible that a few included by him were taken from folklore.

Had Planudius's anthology remained in Greek, the fate of Aesopic fables in the West would have been far less happy than it is. Though we owe much to Planudius, since he saved many fables from virtual oblivion, we owe almost as much to his translator into Latin, one Rinuccio Thesalo or d'Arezzo, who toward the middle of the fifteenth century brought into

Western Europe the first nearly complete anthology of Aesopic material. Some debt is owed, too, to Cardinal Antonio Cerdá of Mallorca, to whom d'Arezzo dedicated his book, for it is likely that this important ecclesiastic did much to publicize Aesop and to aid in the dissemination of d'Arezzo's translation. It may be more than coincidence that Saragossa in the Kingdom of Aragon became a center of Aesopic fables in Spanish so that eventually the *Ysopet* was published there. Lending support to this statement is the fact that d'Arezzo's Latin work was translated into Castilian probably in the 1460s at the behest of Enrique, viceroy of Cataluña under his cousin Ferdinand of Aragon, who married Isabella of Castile. Enrique, to whom the manuscript of the *Ysopet* had been submitted for approval in the 1460s, could not see it printed, since printing did not reach Spain until 1480.

It should be noted that d'Arezzo's translation from the Greek was also translated into other European tongues, but the way in which this affected the course of Aesopic fables in Spain will be treated below. Suffice to say that one important center of translation was Germany.

The work of d'Arezzo in Latin had great success in most of Europe, at least among the erudite, but much less among vernacular speakers whose Latin was weak or nonexistent. Almost as soon as the printing press was invented in Germany vernacular versions of Aesop began to appear. Doctor Heinrich Steinhöwel's translation from d'Arezzo was published by Johannes Zeiner in Ulm and Augsburg at some time between 1474, when printing reached Ulm, and 1483, when it came to Augsburg. The Steinhöwel translation followed the order of fables in d'Arezzo, as might have been expected, and included the lengthy "Life of Aesop," which should be regarded as an important contribution to the rise and development of the European novel. This fictitious biography runs to just over twenty-five pages. It contains a frontispiece illustrating Aesop himself and twenty-eight woodcuts, each depicting an event in his life.

The corpus of fables is divided into eight separate sections variously called "books" or "parts." In the Editio Princeps' table of contents each fable or other form of brief narrative is listed by title. Books I, II, III, and IV contain twenty fables each and are composed of many fables we recognize as belonging to the Aesopic tradition. Book V contains seventeen fables and bears the title *Fabulas extravagantes,* possibly because these stories belong to less familiar collections, such as the *Roman de Renart,* the French *fabliaux,* and folkloric sources. We have labeled this book *The Fanciful Fables of Aesop,* since this is one meaning of *extravagantes.* Book VI also contains seventeen fables and bears the title *Las fabulas de Remicio,* that is, fables of Rinuccio d'Arezzo, a significant fabulist.

Book VII, *Las fabulas de Aviano,* comes from fables written by one Avianus, who flourished sometime between the second and fifth centuries. It contains twenty-seven stories. Book VIII, *Las fabulas collectas de Alfonso e de Poggio y de otros en la forma e orden seguiente,* contains twenty-two. The Alfonso of the title is Petrus Alfonsus, the Aragonese Jew whose twelfth-century *Disciplina Clericalis* was perhaps the most oft quoted of collections. Poggio is Poggio Bracciolini (1380-1459), whose humorous and often scatological *Facetiae* were among the most popular of fable anthologies. We have not been able to identify "los otros" as to source.

In 1489, just six years after the printing in Augsburg, a German printer named Jan Hurus, transplanted to Saragossa, published the Editio Princeps of *La vida del Ysopet con sus fabulas hystoriadas.* Hurus must have known the German version. He had brought the science of printing to Aragon, and he embellished his printing of *Ysopet* with the same woodcuts, or virtually identical copies, printed in the editions of Zeiner in Ulm and Augsburg. One can state, therefore, that the relationship between the German translation of d'Arezzo and the Spanish is remarkably close. The only noticeable difference between the two, insofar as content is concerned, lies in the section entitled "Collectas," in which there are four fables not found in the German text. In a Spanish version of 1496 four more were added. The similarity of the woodcuts and ignorance of the origin of the Spanish translation have led some to believe that the Spanish *Ysopet* was a translation of the German—an obvious error, since both the German and the Castilian were translated from the Latin of d'Arezzo.

Such, in the very briefest terms, is the history of the definitive collections of Aesopic fables in Spain.

The famous woodcuts deserve more attention, for they served not only to enliven the fables and other brief narratives but to fix them in the memories of readers. Narrative art in book illustration had, in medieval times, developed to a remarkable extent. It is not strange, then, that this art continued in the Renaissance in a form not well known in earlier times, that is, in woodcuts, which could be printed as easily as letters. It was primarily in Germany and the Netherlands that this art reached its height. These were the times of Dürer and the "little masters," Aldorfer, Behams, and Pencz, who first began to forsake religious topics in woodcuts to produce, with a touch of the decorative quality learned from Italian masters, the humor and studied debauchery of everyday life.

And so it was that the Editio Princeps of the *Ysopet,* printed in 1489 and made available to thousands, began the centuries-long influence of the greatest fables of the ancient world. From this first volume all the later Spanish editions came, and from this tradition all Spanish writers who mentioned Aesop or used his fables in their works drew their references. It can be stated without fear of contradiction that the romantic life of Aesop and the collection of fables made available to Spaniards in 1489 was the most widely read body of literature across at least two centuries in Spain. Nor should we wonder at this. After all, the same fables from their inception in distant Antiquity until the present, have attracted and held human attention. It is fortunate that the Royal Spanish Academy in 1929 published a complete facsimile of the single extant copy of the Editio Princeps, thereby preserving it for posterity. With the scholarly introduction by Emilio Cotareli y Mori, it contributes vastly to our understanding of a great work of the past.

Today Aesop is read for the pleasure his fables afford rather than for the utilitarian value of their lessons, although these lessons are present, as they were in the fifteenth century and, for that matter, in all the previous centuries. These lessons are universal and are at home in any age and any culture, for they are based upon life itself and the practical wisdom one needs to survive. One can, of course, dispense with the lesson and simply enjoy the stories *per se,* as children do. And yet it may be impossible to divorce *dulce* (story) from *utile* (lesson), because the moralization found in each fable is actually a component of narrative technique perhaps as much as are plot, conflict, characterization, and the other elements of narrative. People expected the moralization, even if they did not always realize they were imbibing it. Moreover, the fables led to the creation of proverbs, which are always a delight and a convenience—even a necessity in daily parlance. In Spain, where proverbs are still a way of life, the *Ysopet* must have generated more of such witty or sententious sayings than anywhere else. In our own daily parlance we seldom pass a day without uttering an "Aesopic proverb," even in abbreviated form, as in "like a dog in the manger," "sour grapes," "cat's paw," and many more.

In the Middle Ages and the Renaissance the Roman Catholic Church allowed Aesopic fables to creep into its sermons and homilies, despite the fact that Aesopic "morality" in its utter utilitarianism was a far cry from the tenets of Christianity. Not even the weak excuse that examples of duplicity and selfishness could be used to teach the avoidance of such qualities actually justified the telling of such fables in the pulpit. The influence of Aesop was everywhere. People heard the fables recited and read them in books, they were depicted in sculpture, in tapestries, in carvings of wood and ivory and stone, they were seen on the capitals of columns and in frescoes and other paintings, and most of all they were familiar in book illustrations.

And today where does one find Aesop? His fables appear in story books for children; some can be found in school books; reciters of folktales include Aesopic fables; in some parts of the world professional tellers or readers offer such fables in their repertories; anthologies like ours in translation contain them; and fables concerned with adultery and cuckoldry, which are not found in true Aesopic fables but are often found accompanying them, have appeared in as popular a magazine as *Playboy* in its "Ribald Classics." Stories in this last category have reached perhaps the largest possible audience, upwards of more than two million subscribers, not counting the many others who read each copy. Aesop's fables are not dead.

The language of *La vida del Ysopet con sus fabulas hystoriadas* is good fifteenth-century Castilian colored somewhat by Aragonese, since it is quite likely that the translator was a native of Aragon. But since translations are often shaped to some degree by the original tongue, specialists may see something not quite typical. They should consider, even so, that a work accepted by a humanist of such consequence as the Viceroy of Cataluña could not have been regarded by him as faulty or dialectal. To the reader of the modern English version none of this is significant, of course. In short, the Spanish from which the present translation was made must have been well received in the Peninsula, to judge by the number of subsequent editions.

The present translation of the *Ysopet* follows to a rather remarkable degree the philosophy of the translator from the Latin, and one may read that interesting concept of the translator's art in the first few lines of the *Ysopet*. The approach to translation taken by the author five hundred years ago and the present-day translators are surprisingly parallel. Modern scholars can improve upon the original, however, and can achieve better success in rendering the imagery, speech, concepts, and thought of the Spanish text. Our parlance is of the most modern American vintage. We have broken up the inordinately lengthy sentences of the original into more manageable form, have created paragraphs, have punctuated where the original did not, and have avoided many of the archaisms and strictures that Hurus's book contained. We believe we have succeeded in offering to modern readers one of the most complete anthologies of Aesopic fables, together with a number of those non-Aesopic tales that by the fifteenth century tended to be included with the true fables. Readers of our translation of *La vida del Ysopet con sus fabulas hystoriadas* are in essence reading what d'Arezzo gave his readers in Latin and therefore what Maximus Planudius offered his readers in Greek.

The Life of Aesop

ere begins the life of Aesop, the very distinguished and clever
fabulist, taken from the Latin and put into Romance, and plainly
and fairly into Spanish. It was translated from Greek into Latin
by Remitius for the very reverend master Antonio, Cardenal
Titular Head of the order of Saint Chrysostomas. With these were fables
which in another time Romulus of Athens, having translated them from
Greek into Latin, sent to his son Tiberinus. And accompanying them are
fables of Avianus, Doligamus, and Alfonso and others, each fable with its
assigned title. They were not rendered word for word, but by seizing the true
sense, as is the common way of interpreters, using clearer and more evident
discussions and clarifications of the text, even frequently adding some words
and rejecting and excluding others in order to provide greater ornamenta-
tion and more honest and profitable eloquence. And this vulgarization and
translation was ordered by and begun under the sponsorship and in the
service of the most excellent and illustrious lord Don Enrique, infante of
Aragon and Sicily, duke of Sogorbe, count of Ampurias and lord of Valdeu-
jon, viceroy of Catalonia. Knowing that the work may not be regarded as
worthy to inform and instruct his enlightened lordship, but because of his
superabundant discretion and most benevolent nobility, we pray it may be
authorized for distribution to the common people and persons less learned
and literate, as, for instance, for a pious father to read to his children.

The aforesaid fables are very profitable if understood by the reader in
connection with the doctrine of Basilius. To do this we must use prudence or,
better still, natural instinct like that of the bees, for they pay little attention
to the apparent color of flowers, but seek the sweetness of the honey and the
usefulness of the wax for building and improving their hive. Yet part of what
they take remains behind, leaving the rest of the flower unharmed. And so
he who desires to read this book should pay no attention to the flowers' color;
that is, he should not heed the fable itself but rather the doctrine contained
in it and understood therein, so as to achieve good habits and virtues; but he
must escape and guard against evil ways by sucking out and deriving

sustenance from the fables for body and soul. For those who do not do so but merely read this book for its fables certainly derive no profit from them but are like the rooster that found a precious stone in the manure pile while looking for food and would have preferred finding a grain of barley or wheat to a precious stone. This is what Aesop's first fable teaches. And as we are to relate some of his fables, it is reasonable to state first what a fable is. It is to be noted that the poets, took this word fable from *defando,* which means "to speak," for fables are things not done but imagined, and they were invented so that by imagining the speech of nonrational animals one to another, the customs and semblances of men might be made known.

The first inventor of fables was called Master Alemocra Coviense. There are various other fables, some called Aesopian, which were written and composed by the very illustrious Aesop, and it is in these that nonrational animals, which have no speech, are introduced. It is pretended that they talk, as well as other objects lacking sense, such as trees, mountains, stones, water, cities, towns, and so forth. Other fables are the so-called Libyan tales, in which men talk to animals and vice versa. The poets too imagined fables because they are pleasant to listen to. They declare and write of the ways of men, by which they are made better, as Terence and Plautus did when they wrote about Vulcan the god of fire as humpbacked and crippled; this is proper to the nature of fire, for the flame of a fire never goes straight up but in twisted fashion.

The poets imagine also a tripartite beast called a chimera, having the head of a lion, the belly of a goat, and the tail of a snake, representing the three states of man; that is to say, youth, manhood, and old age. For men in youth are like the lion, proud, cruel and strong; wherefore, remembering their works in middle age, they are on the lookout for the profitable and flee the unpleasant; wherefore, through their harshness and penetration they are compared with a goat; but in old age, they are constituted like snakes which in various ways they imitate, and so much harm comes to them. The poets also imagine semitaurs and centaurs, which are imagined like men down to the umbilicus and from there down like horses, signifying the brevity of a man's life, which, like the running of the horse, is quickly over. Some customs are approved in this manner, as in Horace's fable in which one mouse tells of having spoken to another and the weasel to a vixen.

These fables were told not because things happened that way but because they reflect the state of men. Thus the fables of Aesop are organized on the model of the lives and customs of men. We have a similar phenomenon in the book of the kings, in which the tree begged for a judge and talked to the olive tree, the fig tree, the grapevine, and the blackberry bush. And all these things are done so that in a figurative way we may achieve the truth we seek. This is what the very illustrious master Demosthenes of Athens did against King Philip when he demanded ten of the most learned citizens of Athens so that the siege of the city might be raised. And he imagined this in a fable: that a wolf asked a shepherd to deliver the mastiffs into his power and he in return would keep peace with the sheep. In so saying he wished to make the citizens of Athens understand that what the king asked is like the situation in Aesop's fable. For Demosthenes said that, just as the wolf asked the shepherd to hand over the dogs so that henceforth he might not fear to eat the sheep, so King Philip asked them to send him the greatest and most learned men in the city so that he might the more easily subjugate them.

Next let us note the difference between a fable, a history, and an argument. Fables are things that are not done and cannot be done, for they would be accomplished outside the confines of nature. Histories are true and come to pass as they are described. Arguments are things that were not made but may be made, like the comedies of Terence and Plautus and similar things. Now let us come to the life of Aesop, which is as follows.

In the region of Phrygia, where the ancient city of Troy was located, there was a small village called Amonia in which was born a deformed boy, ugly of countenance and with a body more deformed than any other boy of his time. He had a large head and piercing black eyes; he was long of jaw and had a twisted neck; he had fat calves and big feet; he was large of mouth, hump-backed and bepaunched; he stuttered, and his name was Aesop. As he grew, in time he surpassed all others in astuteness. He was soon captured and removed to a foreign country, where he was sold to a rich citizen of Athens named Aristes. And as this gentleman thought him useless and of no profit to serve in his house, he assigned him to work and dig in the fields and on his property.

One day Zenas, to whom was entrusted the administration of the property for his lord, arose from his sleep to go to work, as he usually did on the aforesaid lands. In a short while his lord came with a lad named Agathopus. And as Zenas was showing his master how hard he worked, it happened that he came upon a fig tree in which there were a few figs that had ripened earlier than those on the other fig trees. From this tree Zenas carefully picked the figs and presented them with great courtesy to his lordship, saying: "To you belong the first fruits of your land." And the lord, seeing the beauty of the figs, said: "I thank you sincerely, Zenas, for the great affection you have for me."

As it was the time at which he was accustomed on such a day to bathe and cleanse himself, he said: "Oh, Agathopus, take and guard these figs carefully, for when I return from the bath I shall begin my meal with them." But as Agathopus took the figs and looked at them, an uncontrollable urge to gluttony arose within him; he looked again and again at the figs in the presence of one of his comrades, and the two of them together looked at them. And he said: "If I were not afraid of our master I would eat these figs one after another." His companion replied: "I will tell you how to do it in such a way that we will suffer no harm on their account." Agathopus said: "How can this be?" Said the other: "This is easy for us, for Aesop comes every day to get the bread you are accustomed to give him. And when the lord asks for his figs, we will say that Aesop, coming in from his toil and finding the figs in the pantry, ate them. And when Aesop is sent for, with that slowness and stammer of his, he will not be able to defend himself or make any excuse, and the lord will beat him, and we will get what we want." Agathopus, having heard this advice, with his desire for the figs began without further thought to eat, and as he ate them with great pleasure and joy Agathopus said laughing: "Grief and sadness will be your lot, Aesop, for upon your shoulders our lord will furiously avenge our guilt." And so, talking and laughing, they ate up all the figs.

When the lord came from his bath, he asked them to bring him the figs for the first course of his dinner. And Agathopus said: "My Lord, Aesop came from his work and, as he found the pantry open, he went in and, not listening to reason, ate them all." Hearing this, the lord, moved by anger, said: "Who will send for this Aesop for me?" And when Aesop came before the lord, he said to Aesop: "Tell me, mean rascal, shameless one, is this the way you respect me? So little do you fear me that you have had the boldness to eat the figs that were kept in the pantry for me?" Aesop, not being able to answer his master because of his speech impediment, was afraid. And the lord ordered him stripped. But as he was sharp, clever, and astute and knew that he was being falsely accused by those present, he got down on his knees before his master and, making signs, requested a bit of time before he should be beaten, knowing that he could not counter with words the trick his accusers had laid upon him and that he would have to defend himself by cleverness. Whereupon he went to the fire, picked up a pot of hot water he found there, tossed the contents into a basin, and drank it. Then shortly he stuck his fingers into his throat and threw up only the water that he had drunk, for during that day he had had no other food. Then he begged his lord as a favor to have his accusers drink hot water. By command of their lord they drank it, and to keep from vomiting they held their hands to their mouths, but as their stomachs were swollen with hot water they threw up water mixed with figs. And the lord saw plainly, by the experiment, that they had eaten the figs. Turning to them he said: "Because you lied about this man who is not glib, I order you stripped and publicly beaten, that whosoever shall by deceit raise up an accusation against another will have his hide tanned and burnished for a reward."

The following day his lordship went to the city. While Aesop was at his work, digging in the field, there came to him a priest named Ysidis who had strayed from the highway, and he asked Aesop to show him by what road he could reach the city. Being a very pious man, Aesop took him by the hand and had him sit down in the shade of a fig tree and gave him bread and olives and figs and dates and invited him to eat. Then Aesop went to a well and drew water and offered him a drink. After Ysidis had enjoyed himself and rested, Aesop with great kindness showed him the road to the city. And the priest, seeing no way to recompense with money the charity he had received from Aesop, determined to ask the gods and goddesses for a boon for that man who had treated him with such love and affection. When Aesop returned to the fields at the hour of the siesta (for it is the custom of laborers to rest and nap), he fell asleep in the shade of a tree. And as the goddess of piety and charity heard and understood the prayers of Ysidis, she appeared to Aesop and granted him as a boon that he might speak distinctly and without impediment all the languages of people, and understand the songs of birds and the signs of all the animals, and that he might henceforth be the inventor and writer of many fables.

When Aesop awoke from his sleep, he said to himself: "How sweetly I have rested, and methinks I have dreamed a dream of great wonder, and it seems to me that without even trying I am able to speak and can name the things I see by their names, and I am able to understand the songs of birds and recognize signs of animals, and by the gift of the gods I can see and

understand all things. I cannot imagine why I have received this knowledge so suddenly. I think perhaps it is because of the piety, charity, and love I have shown toward strangers on many occasions that the gods have vouchsafed me this boon. He who does good deeds is given hope in his heart always."

While Aesop was enjoying the great boon that he had received from the gods, he took up his spade and began to dig again in the field. But when Zenas came along to look at his work and see what he had accomplished, he was overcome with anger, and without reason he struck one of Aesop's companions with his staff. Aesop, angry at this action, said: "Why for no reason do you strike this man? You are always hitting us without reason and striking us to hurt us. You do no decent action. I shall certainly see to it that this cruelty of yours is made known to our master." When Zenas heard Aesop's words he marveled to hear him speak so distinctly and contradict him without difficulty, and he said to himself: "I'll have to take steps before this rascal gets me in trouble with our master and deprives me of my power." Then he went off to the city and began to talk to his master, putting up a good front and saying: "May you enjoy good health, My Lord." And the lord replied: "Why do you come to me trembling?" Zenas answered: "A marvel has happened on your land." The lord replied: "Is it perchance that some fruit tree has borne fruit before its time, or has one of the animals given birth to a monster?" And Zenas said: "No, it's nothing like that, but that wicked, criminal slave Aesop has begun to talk clearly and without impediment." Then the lord said: "This is a fine thing, which seems to you monstrous and contrary to nature." And Zenas said: "That is no marvel. We often see men who lose their reason and find themselves unable to speak, and when the madness leaves them they say anything they like without difficulty or hindrance." Then Zenas said: "He says more than a man; he said insulting words to me about you and about the gods and goddesses. He blasphemes cruelly and falsely." And the lord, moved by anger, said to Zenas: "Go and do what you like with him. You must strike him and sell him and destroy him. I'll give him to you and make you a donation of him in writing." And Zenas, having accepted and received the gift, returned to the field and said to Aesop: "Now you are in my power, for our master has given you to me. And because you speak evil in every way, I intend to sell you."

It happened by chance that a merchant who was accustomed to buying slaves was passing near the field looking for animals for hire to carry loads and slaves to the fair at Ephesus. And when the merchant met Zenas, whom he knew, he greeted him and asked him if he knew of any animals for sale or hire. Zenas said: "Not for any price or in any fashion do I know of animals here, but I have a very learned slave of profitable age, and I will sell him if you want to buy him." The merchant said: "I'd like to see him." Then Zenas called Aesop and showed him to the merchant who, seeing his homeliness, said: "Where is this freak from? He looks certainly like the chief herald of battle of the monsters and marvels. If he were speechless I would think him a bloated drunkard. Did you take me out of my way for the sake of this bundle of filth? I thought I was coming to buy a learned slave, that is, a handsome and elegant one." Having said this he started on his way.

But Aesop followed the merchant and said to him: "Wait a minute!" "Don't waste my time," replied the merchant, "for you cannot be useful to me in any way. If I bought you they would call me a buyer of oddities or of marvels and monsters." And Aesop said to him: "Well, why did you come here?" And the buyer answered, "Certainly I came thinking I might buy a gentle slave, but you are too dirty and ugly. Such merchandise I do not need." And Aesop said, "You have nothing to lose by buying me." Then the merchant said to Aesop: "How could you be useful to me?" Aesop replied: "Have you not in your place of residence some inexperienced and bashful boys or young men? Buy me and put me in charge of them. For in truth they will be more afraid of me than of a scarecrow." Hearing these words, the merchant went back excitedly to Zenas and asked: "How much do you want for this bundle of rags?" "Three gold coins or thirty pieces of silver," said Zenas "for I know that nobody will want him for merchandise, and so I am giving him to you for practically nothing."

The merchant paid the price and took Aesop home with him. When he came into his house with Aesop, there were two boys seated on their mother's lap, and when the children saw Aesop they were frightened and began to cry and hide their faces in their mother's bosom. Then Aesop said to his master: "Now you have the proof and argument of my promise. For you perceive that as soon as the children saw me they decided I was a devil or scarecrow." The merchant laughed at Aesop's reply and then said: "Come in and greet your fellow slaves." Aesop went in and saw the handsome and estimable slave boys, and he said: "God keep you, my good companions." And they looked at Aesop and said: "By the dark sun, we were expecting a spectacle and a wonder. What is our master doing? Up to now he has never bought so ugly a creature." And while they were there the master came into the room where they were gathered and said to the lads: "Mourn your fate! For I found no animals for sale or rent. Divide the loads among yourselves, and take food with you, for tomorrow we are going to Ephesus."

As the boys were dividing the burdens, share and share alike, Aesop said: "Good companions, you know that I am the smallest and weakest among you. I beg you, give me something light." And they replied: "Since you cannot carry a full load, do not carry anything at all." And Aesop said: "Since you are all working, it is not right for me alone to remain useless and unprofitable to our master." And they replied: "Take whatever you like." Aesop looked at what there was to carry on the road, that is, sacks, baggage, and baskets, and he picked up a basket full of bread, which was a load big enough for two men, and said to them: "I'll take this load." They said: "There is no one crazier than this man. He asks us for a light load and picks up the heaviest one." And one of them said: "Let us load him as usual." So Aesop took the bread on his back and walked faster than the other slaves. And they, looking at him, marveled at it and said: "This fellow is not lazy in his work. Truly he is carrying a heavier burden than the rest of us. By this alone he is earning what he cost, for a good beast of burden could not carry more." And in this manner they made fun of Aesop because no two of them carried so large a load as he alone. But when they came to a hill Aesop took the load off his back and laid it on the ground, and gripping it with his hands and teeth he climbed the hill with less difficulty. And so he was received at the inn before the others.

When they all reached the inn the master ordered them to rest a while and take some recreation. And he said to Aesop: "Bring some bread and give it to these men to eat." Aesop gave out so much bread to each one that the basket was left about half empty. They rose from their meal, and Aesop with his lightened burden reached the next inn before the rest of them. That night in similar fashion he divided the bread among his companions and so emptied the whole basket. The next day, as they were getting up early, Aesop went on ahead of the rest with his empty basket so that they could not recognize him because of the distance between them. And the slaves, looking at him, not realizing it was Aesop, said to each other: "Who is that so far ahead of us? Is it one of our company or some pilgrim? Don't you see how this sharp fellow has beaten us all in subtlety and astuteness? For we took loads that are not used up on the way, and we toil as we go, while this clever fellow loaded himself up with bread which is used up each day, and now he goes along as you see without any load, taking it easy."

When they reached Ephesus the merchant sent the slaves to be sold to the market and made a considerable profit from them. Three slaves alone were left unsold. These were a grammarian, a musician, and Aesop. Someone who knew the merchant said: "If you take these slaves to a place called Samun, you will be able to sell them there. A philosopher lives there named Xanthus to whom resort many young men from the renowned Cyclades and the Esporades Islands to learn as they study." Having heard this, the merchant sailed to Samun, and after dressing the musician and the grammarian in new clothes, put them up for sale in the market. And Aesop, because he looked very languid and ugly, he placed between the two of them, dressed only in sackcloth. As the other two were handsome and well proportioned, everyone who looked at Aesop was frightened at his ugliness and said: "And where did this ridiculous clown come from? Certainly he beats them all in ugliness and ungainly frame." But Aesop, knowing he was being made fun of and sneered at, was annoyed and looked at everyone threateningly. And as the philosopher Xanthus came out of his house to the market and walked by idly, looking up and down, he saw those two handsome, well built lads with Aesop between them. Marveling at the vendor's ignorance he said: "What a man of wisdom!" And coming up to one of the slaves he asked him where he was from. The slave answered that he was a native of Cappadocia. And Xanthus said to him: "What can you do?" the slave said: "I'll do whatever you like." Hearing this reply, Aesop laughed

very cynically, and to the scholars who were with the philosopher, seeing
Aesop laugh and grin as he did, he looked like a monster outside the human
condition. They said among themselves: "Why, has this belly teeth?" And
one of them said: "Why did he laugh so loudly?" And the other said, "He is
not laughing but grumbling. Let's ask him to tell us the reason." One of them
went up to Aesop and said to him: "Learned fellow, tell me why you laughed
so heartily." Aesop, angry at being made fun of by everyone, replied: "Go
away with bad luck, you animal, you sea goat." And at this outburst the
scholar was embarrassed and took himself away.

But the philosopher said to the merchant: "What will you sell the
musician for?" To which the merchant replied, "For three thousand pieces of
money." And as this price seemed a bit high, the philosopher went to the
other slave and said to him: "What country are you from?" To which he
replied: "I am from Lydia." And the philosopher said: "What can you do?"
And the slave said: "I'll do whatever occurs to you." Hearing this, Aesop
laughed heartily. And the scholars, seeing him laugh, said: "Why does this
fellow laugh at everything?" And one of them said: "If you want to be called a
sea goat ask him why he is laughing." Xanthus said to the merchant: "How
much do you want for the grammarian?" And he answered: "Three thousand
pieces of money." Hearing this the philosopher was silent and walked away.
Then the scholars said: "Master, do those two slaves please you or don't
they?" "Yes, they please me, but we are forbidden to spend so much money
for a servant. And the buyer of them would be penalized." "Well," they said,
"since the two handsome ones cannot be bought because of the rule, buy the
one whom no one can exceed or overtake in ugliness, for certainly he will

serve you no worse than another. We will pay the price for him." The philosopher replied: "That would be a bad business. Besides, my wife is delicate and would not allow herself to be served by such a man." The two students spoke up again: "Master, you have given us many commands and teachings to which women would not consent except to be contrary, and that is the way you should treat them." Then the philosopher said: "Let us find out what he can do so as not to waste the purchase price through carelessness." Returning to Aesop he said to him: "God keep you, lad." Aesop replied: "I beg you, don't trouble yourself with me." Xanthus said: "I greet you." And Aesop replied: "And I you." Then the philosopher said to him: "Lay aside your irritation and annoyance and answer my questions. From what country do you come?" Aesop answered: "Of flesh." Xanthus said: "That is not what I am asking you, but where you were conceived." Aesop replied: "In my mother's womb." And the philosopher answered: "That is not what I am asking you either. But in what place were you born?" And Aesop answered: "My mother did not tell me in what room she gave birth to me, whether in the bedroom or in the drawing room."

Xanthus said: "Let us leave this; tell me what you have learned." And Aesop replied: "I do not know how to do anything." Xanthus asked him: "In what way do you say that?" "I declare it," said Aesop, "because my fellow slaves declared that they knew how to do all sorts of things and so they left nothing for me to claim." Then the students, marveling, said to each other, "By the divine knowledge, he answered well. A person who knows all things is not to be found, and that is why he laughed so loudly." The philosopher said to him: "I want you to tell me whether you want me to buy you." Aesop said: "That is up to you. Certainly no one is forcing you to, but if you feel like it, open your purse and count the money; if not, close it." Having heard these things the two scholars said: "By the gods, this fellow surpasses the master." The philosopher asked Aesop to tell him whether, if he bought him, he would run away. Aesop replied: "If I wanted to do so I wouldn't ask your advice." Xanthus said: "You answer very honestly, but you are misshapen and very ugly." Aesop replied: "No one should look at the outward appearance, but at the soul and heart of a man." Then the philosopher said to the merchant: "How much do you want for this scarecrow?" The latter said: "Wait a minute. Certainly you know very little about merchandise." Xanthus asked: "Why do you say things like that?" The merchant replied: "Because you pass over those who are worthy of you and take the unworthy one. Take one of those and leave this one." Xanthus replied: "I am asking for how much will you give him to me?" "Sixty pieces of money," said the merchant. Then the scholars counted out the price, and in this manner the philosopher acquired Aesop.

The brokers when they learned of this sale, earnestly demanded to know who had been the seller and who the buyer. But the philosopher and the merchant agreed as one man to keep to themselves that it had been a low price. But Aesop said to the brokers: "This is the buyer and this is the seller, and if both deny it I am free, and as such I declare myself." And for this bit of cleverness the brokers, smiling at this deal, thought the reproof deserved. And each one took off in the direction in which he wanted to go, and Aesop followed his master, Xanthus.

It happened that his lord urinated as he walked along. Seeing this, Aesop plucked at Xanthus's garment and said: "My lord, if you do not sell me to another, I am telling you that I shall run away." "Why is that?" asked Xanthus. Aesop said: "I cannot serve such a master." The philosopher asked: "Why not?" Aesop replied: "Because you are not ashamed, though an honorable gentleman, to urinate while walking along. Can't you give nature her due and urinate standing still? According to this, I, your slave, if you sent me to do something and my bowels required voiding, should have to do it on the run as you do that which is ill done when you do it while proceeding on your way." The philosopher replied: "I beg of you, do not be upset on account of this, but open your ears to what I shall tell you. I urinate while walking to avoid three unpleasant things: The first is the heat of the sun; as it is midday, I do so in order not to sunburn my head; the second is in order that the urine may not burn my feet; and third is so that the odor of the urine may not offend my nose. And by urinating while walking I avoid these three offenses." "Then," said Aesop, "you have satisfied me."

When the philosopher reached his house he said to Aesop: "Stay here by the door for a bit while I go to the study and to your mistress to tell her about you." Aesop said: "I shall not wait for you at all, but I will do as you command." Xanthus went into the house and said to his wife: "From now on you will cease to differ with me and to quarrel with me for saying that I require the use of your servant boys. Take notice that I have bought you a lad than whom I have seen no one more learned up to now, nor more handsome, nor genteel." The female slaves, as soon as they heard this, believing it was true, began to contend and argue with each other. One said: "The master has bought him for me for a husband." Another said: "I dreamt last night that my lord had betrothed me to him." And while they were talking, his wife said to Xanthus: "Where is this fellow whom you praise so highly? Tell him to come here." And the philosopher said: "He is at the door. Tell someone to have the newly purchased lad come up." And one of the female slaves, while the others argued as to who should call him, went after him and said to herself silently: "I will be the first and will take him for a husband." As soon as she got to the door she began to say: "Where is the one for whom I hope?" And Aesop replied: "I am the one you are asking for." When she looked at him she changed color, was frightened, and said: "Woe is me, I will flee and distance myself from this phantom! Where is his tail?" And Aesop answered: "If it's a tail you want you will not lack for one." As he tried to come into the house the servant said: "You shall not enter here, for if you do, all who are inside will flee when they see you." And after she had returned to her companions who wanted to see him, she said: "I to my sorrow saw him there, so you may go and see him." Another, going out as if to look at Aesop, who was so ugly and frightful, said to him: "Your sharp tongue will cut your mouth; be careful not to touch me." And Aesop presented himself before his mistress, entering as it were his own house. But as she looked at him, she turned and said to her husband: "So you have bought me a scarecrow and a monster for a slave. Take him away." The philosopher replied: "Woman, soften your heart! For I have bought him for your servant. He is even fairly satisfactory and a man of learning." And she said to him: "I am not so stupid as not to realize that you now abhor me and are looking for another wife. Why don't you come out and say so openly? It is for this reason that you have brought me this dog's head, thinking that I would prefer to leave home rather than converse with him. But since things are as they are, give me my dowry and I'll leave peacefully."

And Xanthus said to Aesop: "When we were on the road you did a lot of talking, and now when you ought to talk you are silent and say nothing." Aesop answered him: "Sir, since this wife of yours is of such a proud and haughty disposition, abandon her to the devil." And Xanthus said: "Be quiet. You are fit to be whipped. Don't you see that I love her as I love myself?" "And no less," replied Aesop. "I beg you to love her," said Xanthus, "more than anyone else." Then Aesop stamped his way into the parlor and said in a loud voice: "This philosopher is taken with this woman." And returning to the lady he began to speak as follows, "I will love you and work

for you, my lady, so that you may have peace and well-being. You would have preferred to have your husband purchase you a young man for a slave, handsome in appearance, learned, elegant, and well dressed, who would wait on you at the bath and minister to you in bed, take care of your feet, and who, when you desire it, would confound the philosopher, who said 'There is suffering in the perils of the sea, oh, thou of golden speech and false in nothing.' And the best word he spoke is: 'Numerous are the convulsions and upheavals of the sea and very frequent are the surgings and turbulence of streams. A hard thing it is to bear poverty, and truly there is an infinite number of evil things to suffer and endure, but the worst is to tolerate an evil woman.' But you, madame, do not want handsome and lusty young men to serve you, since in a short time you might bring dishonor and infamy to your husband."

The mistress heard all these things and said: "He is not only ugly and deformed but talkative and an inventor of cruelties. With what words does he make fun of me and scorn me! But I will hold my temper and will change my ways." Then the philosopher said, "Note well, Aesop, that the lady is angry." Aesop replied, "The power to tame and please a woman is not given easily."

Then the lord ordered Aesop to be quiet, saying: "Be silent now, for you have said enough. Take a basket and follow me so that we may buy some greens." So they went to a garden, and the philosopher said to the gardener, "Give us some greens." The gardener took a bundle in which there were kale and other greens together and gave it to Aesop, and as his lord paid the price and began to walk on, the gardener said to him: "I ask you, master, to wait a

minute, for I would like to ask you a question." The philosopher said: "I am
willing. I will gladly wait for you. Say what you like." And the gardener said:
"Master, why is it that the herbs and vegetables that are diligently sown and
worked with great care develop later than those which grow by themselves
and are not worked." And Xanthus, when he heard this philosophical question and could not answer it, said: "Such things proceed from divine providence." At this Aesop laughed merrily, and his lord said to him: "You are
mad to laugh, or are you joking." Said Aesop: "I am not mocking you but the
philosopher who taught you. And what kind of philosophic solution is it to
say that these things have their origin in divine providence? These things
the saddle makers know." Said Xanthus: "Well, you tackle the question."
Aesop replied: "Well, if you command me, it is easy to do."

Then the master turning to the gardener said: "It is not proper for a
philosopher who continually teaches in the curriculum to answer in a
garden and to solve riddles. But this lad, who is learned in these matters,
will resolve the question if I ask him to." And the gardener said: "Does this
dirty fellow know his letters? Oh, what a misfortune!" And he said to Aesop:
"And you, lad, do you know these things?" To which Aesop replied: "I think
so, but pay attention. You ask why the plants you sow and cultivate grow
more slowly than those that sow themselves and are not cultivated. Open
your ears and listen! It is like the case of a widow woman who has sons and
marries a second husband who has children. To some she is mother and to
others stepmother, and there is a great difference between the stepchildren
and those of the first marriage. For the children are brought up with great
care and affection and the stepchildren are treated with negligence and even

with abhorrence. In this fashion the earth is the mother of the plants that grow by themselves. And to the others, which are sown by the hand of man, she is a stepmother." And when the gardener heard these things, he said: "You have saved me from a great preoccupation. I gladly give you the greens, and when you need some come and take anything you like from the garden."

Three days later, as the philosopher was taking a bath together with other members of his family and friends, he commanded Aesop: "Go to the house and put a lentil dish in a pot as quickly as you can and cook it." Aesop went running, and going into the room he took a single lentil and threw it into the pot to cook, and got everything that was necessary and proper. After they had bathed, Xanthus said to his friends: "Today you will eat lentils with me. You must not look at the value of this food but at the good will with which it is offered." And when he came to lunch the master ordered Aesop: "Bring us water for our hands." Then, taking the foot bath, Aesop went to the privy and filled it with water and brought it to his master. The master, smelling the bad smell, said: "What is this, you wicked fellow. You are mad. Take that away and bring us the basin." Aesop quickly brought the empty basin, and the philosopher said with annoyance: "Lad, you know better than that." He answered: "By you I was once told not to bring anything but what was asked for. You did not say to put water in the basin or wash your feet, or prepare the towels and napkins and the other things that are necessary. You only said: 'Bring the basin,' and I brought it." Then the philosopher said to his friends, "I didn't buy a servant, but a master and ruler."

As they were sitting at the table Aesop's lord told him that if the lentils were ready, to bring them in. Aesop took a spoon and removed the lentil he had placed in the pot and brought it to the table. And the master, thinking he had brought it so that they might see whether the lentils were cooked, broke the lentil with his fingers, and said: "It is cooked. Bring them and we will eat them." Aesop then placed upon the table a platter of meat only, and Xanthus said: "What has become of the lentils?" Aesop answered: "I brought it to you on a spoon." The master said: "It is true that it is a lentil, but I said a lentil dish." Aesop said: "You ordered me to cook a lentil dish in the singular and not lentils in the plural." Disturbed in heart, the master said to those who were at the table: "Certainly this fellow will drive me mad." Then he said to Aesop: "If you do not want me to become a laughing-stock to my friends, go and buy four pig's feet, cook them quickly, and put them on the table." Aesop went and bought them and put them to cook in a pot. And the lord, seeking a reason to whip him, took a pig's foot out of the pot and hid it while Aesop was tending to other matters. So when Aesop in a little while looked into the pot, he found only three pig's feet. Imagining how the thing had happened, he went down to the stable and cut a foot off the pig that was there, returned upstairs, and put it in the pot. But Xanthus was afraid that Aesop, not finding the pig's foot, might flee for fear of a beating. So while Aesop was below he returned the pig's foot to the pot. And when the pig's feet were cooked, and when he had emptied the pot onto a plate, Aesop brought up five pig's feet, and Xanthus, when he saw them, said: "What is this? Perhaps a pig with five feet?" And Aesop said: "And how many feet do two pigs have?" Xanthus said: "Eight." "Well, here are five," said Aesop. "And the pig down below has only three feet." Then Xanthus said to his friends: "Peradventure did I not say that this fellow would drive me mad, and out of my mind?" And Aesop said: "Do you know, my lord, that all things that are done are said in a manner other than what judgment and good reason dictate are not moderate or virtuous?" Then the philosopher, having no just cause to whip him, let it pass, hiding his feelings.

Another day, as the scholars were in the auditorium where Xanthus was reading, one of them prepared dinner. And as they were eating, Xanthus took a portion of the meat and gave it to Aesop saying: "Come here and take this to my loving one, and give it to her." On the way Aesop said to himself: "Now the occasion has arisen for my lady to avenge herself for the things I said to her. And it will now seem clear that the master wishes her well." And so, going into the house, he sat down with those of the house and, calling the lady by name, put forward the basket containing the meat and said: "My lady, you shall taste of none of these meats." And she said: "You always act crazy and do mad things." Aesop replied: "These meats Xanthus did not order given to you but to his well-loving one." And calling to the bitch that was always in the house he said: "Come here, greedy one, and fill your stomach with these meats." And the bitch, wagging her tail with joy, came to

the odor of the meats, and Aesop gave her the meats bone by bone. "The lord
said that to you, and to no other, should these meats be given." Afterwards
he returned to the philosopher, who said: "Did you give the meats to my well-
loving one." Aesop replied: "I gave them to her and before my eyes she ate
them all." Xanthus asked: "And what did she say while she was eating?"
And Aesop replied: "Certainly she said nothing. But it seemed that she loved
you and desired you." But seeing this, Xanthus's wife came into the room
weeping and complaining.

After the scholars had eaten and drunk copiously on the one hand and
on the other, each one asked questions. And one of them asked what time
would be of the greatest urgency and difficulty to men. Aesop, quick in his
wit, said: "He who stands behind the others at the Resurrection when each of
the dead will be looking for his body." Having heard this, the scholars said:
"Certainly this lad is sharp and not inept or deranged in mind. He is more
open and clearly more learned than his lord." Afterward another one asked
why animals brought to slaughter are silent and do not give voice, while the
pig not only lets himself be taken but continually grunts and squeals. As
before, Aesop answered: "As herds of animals like cows and sheep and other
animals are used to being milked and sheared, they come quietly, for they
think they are being summoned for that reason, and so they are not afraid of
the knife, but in the case of the pig, for whose wool and milk we have no
desire, since we are only accustomed to eat its flesh and blood, when they
bring him in he readily grunts and squeals." Then the scholars together
praised and approved what Aesop said and went away happy and pleased to
their homes.

The master, coming home and getting into bed, began to comfort his wife, who was weeping. She, turning her face away, said: "Go away and keep your hand still." The philosopher cajoled and persuaded her, saying: "You are my delight and it is not fitting for you to be angry and sad toward me, your husband." But she answered that he should send her away, as she did not wish to be with him anymore. And she said to her husband: "Call the bitch and praise her to whom you sent the meat." As he did not know what it was all about, he said: "What did Aesop bring you from the banquet?" She answered: "He did not bring me anything." The philosopher said: "Peradventure I am drunk, for certainly I sent you your share by Aesop." She said: "To me?" "To you." She answered: "You did not send it to me, but to the bitch, so Aesop said." Then Xanthus said: "Send for that slave." Aesop came immediately and his master said to him: "To whom did you give the meat?" And he answered: "To your well-loving one, as you commanded." Then Xanthus said to his wife: "Perhaps you hear well what Aesop said." She answered: "I hear it. But I say it again and I repeat, he brought nothing for me but something for the bitch only." And the lord said to Aesop: "To whom did you give it, gallowsbird?" He replied: "To whom you commanded." The lord said: "I ordered you to take them to my well-loving one." And Aesop answered: "And so I brought them to your well-loving one. For the woman you love does not love you at all, for in a very small thing you offend her, then she discovers it and says as much evil as she can and gets angry and leaves home. The bitch, even though you strike her and mistreat her, never leaves you. But when the lord calls her again, with her tail between her legs she comes and fawns on you and flatters you. Therefore you ought to have said: 'Take it to my wife and not to the one who loves me well.'"

Then Xanthus said: "You see, wife, whether it was my fault or that of the messenger. But I beg you to calm yourself, for I shall find a reason to strike him and shall whip him with reason." She said: "Do as you like with him, for nothing will happen to me from now on." So she waited a while and then left the house secretly and went to the home of her relatives. When her husband learned of his wife's departure he was angered and saddened by it. And Aesop said to him: "Now you see that it is not she but your bitch who really loves you." As she did not return home for some days, the husband suffered gravely, and it was hard for him. He sent to ask her to come home, and she, not wishing to obey her husband and being obstinate and hardheaded from day to day, said: "Never more will I return to him."

But Aesop said to Xanthus: "Sir, cheer up, for I shall certainly bring it about that she of herself, without being sent for, will come running home." And he took some money and went the next day to the market and bought chickens and capon and peacocks and geese, and then passing through the street where his lord's wife was, pretending that he did not know where she was, asked a servant coming out of the house where she was that he might sell her some fowls and other things for a wedding that was to be held in town. And the slave asked him who was getting married. Aesop replied: "The philosopher, Xanthus, is taking a wife tomorrow and is celebrating with a big wedding." Hearing this, the slave entered the house and told everything to Xanthus's wife who, very quickly and very much upset and crying, went to the house of the philosopher, her husband, entered the house, and said: "This is why you scorned me through that ill-willed slave. But you will not do as you intend, for while I am alive that other woman will not enter this house, and this I say to you, Xanthus."

A few days later, as Xanthus was inviting his disciples to lunch, he said to Aesop: "You must buy what is good, sweet and savory." And Aesop, as he was going to the market, said to himself: "Now I will demonstrate that I do not know how to prepare a luncheon." He went to the meat market and bought only hog's tongues, which he cooked and put on the table. The philosopher and his disciples, when they sat down, told Aesop to bring in the food. And Aesop put the tongues on the table, with salt and vinegar, and the disciples, praising the master, said: "Sir, this luncheon is full of philosophy." Then in a little while Xanthus ordered Aesop to bring in some other meat. Again he brought tongue, fixed with pepper and garlic sauce. Then the scholars said: "Master, rightfully was the tongue placed on the table, for one tongue sharpens another." A little later the master said to Aesop: "Bring here some other meat." And he brought tongue again, and the guests, now disturbed, talked about it. Already tired of it, they said: "And how long will the tongue last?" The philosopher, moved by anger, said: "Haven't we perchance anything else to eat?" And Aesop replied: "Certainly there is nothing else." And Xanthus said: "Oh, you wicked fellow. I shall not fail to whip you! Buy something good, sweet, and savory." Aesop replied: "That's what you ordered, but I thank the gods that the men here now are philosophers. But I would like you to tell me what is better or sweeter than tongue. Because certainly every doctrine and every art and philosophy is established and ordered by tongue. That is to say: to give, to take, to greet, judgment, merchandise, glory, sciences, weddings, houses, cities—all by tongues are made. By tongues do men exalt themselves. In the tongue consists and is almost all the life of mortals. Thus, as there is nothing better or sweeter than the tongue, you will find nothing more salutary that has been given by the immortals to mortals than the tongue." Then the scholars, embracing Aesop, said: "Aesop speaks well, for it seems, master, that you were mistaken in thinking this was meant otherwise and was wicked."

The next day, the master, eager to excuse himself before his disciples, said to them: "Yesterday you did not dine as I commanded but according to this worthless slave. Today we shall change the viands. For I shall command him to do what he should have done before." And having called Aesop he said to him: "Bring us the worst and most meager thing you can find for dinner, for these men are to eat with me." Nevertheless Aesop, quite without fear, went to the butcher shop and, as before, bought tongue and cooked it and prepared it in the same manner. And when in the afternoon the scholars sat down to eat, Xanthus said to Aesop: "Bring in the meal." The slave put the tongue on the table as before, with the same kind of sauce. Then the scholars said: "Here we go with tongue again." And he brought tongue again. At this those who were to dine grew indignant and did not take the matter patiently. Then the philosopher said to Aesop: "Did I not tell you yesterday to bring the best and sweetest? Then today I told you to bring the worst and most meager, and that was my command." Aesop replied: "Very true are the things you say, but I ask you if you can find anything worse or more stinking than tongue. All men perish by the tongue; by the tongue men come into poverty; by the tongue cities are destroyed. All evil comes from the tongue." Then one of the men who was seated at the table said to Xanthus: "If you look at this fellow and heed him, you will certainly end up in extreme folly, for as his body is, so is his heart." And Aesop said: "You are a sharp goad. And much do you goad the master against the servant. Furthermore you are curious and sharper than the rest."

And Xanthus, seeking a reason to flog Aesop, said to him: "Well, you call the philosopher curious and anxious; show me a man who is without care." And leaving the house, Aesop looked about and tried to find a man who was carefree, and he looked at many whom he encountered. He saw a peasant, to whom he said: "The philosopher, my master, invites you to eat with him." The peasant, not caring to ask why he was invited by a man he did not know, followed Aesop confidently, and with his muddy shoes entered the house without a care and sat down at the table with the rest. Then Xanthus said to his wife: "How can I reasonably strike and whip Aesop? And so, because the others are indeed quicker to obey us, receive patiently what I shall tell you and do not let it annoy you." Then he said aloud: "My lady, take the basin of water and wash the feet of this pilgrim," thinking that the peasant, embarrassed by this, would leave the house and for that reason Aesop would be whipped. The wife, as her husband commanded, put the

basin at the feet of the rustic, and he, knowing that she was the lady of the house, said to himself thoughtfully: "Why does this man wish to honor me so greatly? Not commanding the servants, male or female, he orders his wife to wash my feet." And so he allowed his feet to be washed, and well washed, and was pleased. Then the philosopher ordered his wife that she herself should give him to drink. And the rustic said to himself: "Although it is proper for them to drink first, since it is the will of this honorable gentleman I shall obey his commands." And picking up the glass he drank boldly. As they were eating, the philosopher put a fish before him, telling him to eat, and the rustic, free from embarrassment, ate it with gusto and pleasure. The philosopher seeing this ordered the cook sent for and said to him: "This fish is not well presented and cooked," and he ordered him stripped and beaten. And the rustic said to himself, "There is no sauce lacking to this fish, and so they whipped this fellow without reason. But what is it to me if the cook is whipped or not? I'll fill my belly with good viands and let the cook avenge himself." And Xanthus, seeing the invited guest eating the fish, stopped speaking.

Afterward the rustic began to cut the bread they brought to the table in large pieces like bricks, and Xanthus, not looking at it, began to eat. As the philosopher looked at the rustic and saw how he was eating with gusto and great enthusiasm, he called the baker and said to him: "You dirty rascal, why didn't you put honey or pepper in this bread?" The baker answered: "If this bread is mine and not well made, punish me even to the point of death, and if it isn't my bread, your wife is at fault and not I." Xanthus said: "If this is my wife's fault, I'll have her burned alive." Turning to his wife, who was silent, he told her to say nothing, so that he might flog Aesop. And he ordered one of the servants: "Take some vine shoots into the privy and light a fire. And you, Aesop, take this wife of mine and make a fire there to burn her." All this the philosopher pretended, thinking that the rustic, on hearing these remarks, would get up and wish to prevent the deed. But the rustic said to himself: "This fellow intends to burn his wife without reason." And he said to Xanthus: "Sir, I beg that if you wish to burn your wife, wait a bit until I bring mine so that both may be burned together." Hearing this and marveling, Xanthus said to himself: "Stouthearted is this man, and he is carefree indeed." Returning to Aesop he said: "It is obvious that you have gotten the better of me. But henceforth I will not be like this. If you serve me faithfully and with diligence, you will win your freedom." Aesop replied: "This I will do in all things continually, so that you may not rightfully bear judgment against me."

Three days later the philosopher said to Aesop: "See if there are many men in the public bath, for if there are not many there, I should like to go there to bathe." And Aesop, on going there, met the mayor of the city who, knowing that he was a slave of Xanthus, said to him: "Where are you going, jokester?" Aesop replied: "I'm not sure." The mayor, thinking he was trying to be funny, ordered him carried off to jail. And Aesop, being a captive, said: "Mr. Mayor, I spoke the truth to you, that I did not know where I was going, for a while ago I little thought that I would go to jail a prisoner." And for these words the judge ordered him set free. Wherefore Aesop, going to the bath, where there was a great throng, saw that all who came in and went out hurt their feet on a stone. Finally a man who was seated at the door of the bath, as he struck his foot upon the stone, removed it and put it aside. When Aesop saw this, he went home and said to his lord that there was a single man at the bath, and so the philosopher said to him, "Take these necessities and let's go to the bath." On entering the bath he saw a great number of people and angrily said to Aesop: "Why, you misshapen rogue, did you not say that there was in the bath but a single man?" To which Aesop replied: "That's what I said. And among them there is but a single man. If you will listen to me you will see that I spoke the truth. That stone which is in the corner was, when I came here, in the doorway, and everyone who went in stubbed his toes on it, and there was but one of them who removed it and put it where you now see it, and he is the only one whom I call a man, and not the others." Then the philosopher said: "You did not take long to make excuses." After Xanthus came out of the bath, refreshed, having reached his house, he relieved himself, Aesop being present with the expected jug of water so that he might wash. And Xanthus asked Aesop: "Tell me why when they go out to relieve themselves men look at their stool." Aesop replied: "Formerly as a learned man seated in a private place relieved himself, taking pleasure in it he took his time and he cast out his brains and marrow from his mind together with the scum or dross, and from that time, men, for fear of a

similar happening, when they relieve themselves, always look at their stool. But cease to fear that, for what you don't have you need not fear to lose."

On another day, when Xanthus was sitting with his friends and holding a glass in his hand, troubled by many and diverse questions that were proposed to him, Aesop said to him: "Lord, it can be read in a book by Dionysius that a glass held in company contains three forces. The first force is delight, the second joy, and the third madness. Therefore I ask you, Sir, to drink happily and let other things alone." To this Xanthus, drunk with wine, said: "Silence, you voice of hell and darkness!" Aesop replied: "Since you were in hell, be careful not to avenge yourself upon me." One of the scholars, hearing that Xanthus was overcome with wine, said to him: "Tell me, Master, could a man alone drink up the whole ocean?" The philosopher replied: "And why not? I alone could drink up the whole sea." And the disciple said: "And if you don't drink it all, what will you pay?" Xanthus replied: "I will give up my house if I do not drink it." And they made a bet on this, putting up their rings in sign of good faith, and each one went home.

The next morning Xanthus got up and washed his face, and not seeing the ring on his hand he asked Aesop: "Do you know anything about my ring?" He said: "No, Sir, but I am certain that we will soon have a guest in the house." Xanthus said to him: "Why do you say that?" Aesop replied: "Because yesterday you made a bet that you would drink up the sea, and for a pledge you left your ring." Xanthus, startled when he heard this, said: "In what fashion could I drink up the whole sea? It cannot be." And Aesop said: "Well, that is the way it is." Xanthus said: "I beg of you, see if by your wit you can help me with your counsel to see if I can win, and, if not, how to get out of the bet." Aesop said: "You can't win, but you can get free of and untangle the bet." Xanthus said to him: "Show me how it can be done." Aesop said: "This is the way and the manner of it: When you deny it, they will require you to hand over what you promised; you will then ask them to place furniture and a table for you on the seashore, and to place there cup-bearing servants with all the equipment necessary for the purpose, and you will see the townsfolk gathered together. Have the cups, pitchers, and jars washed in the sea. Then, holding the glass in your hand full of water and salt, order, according to the agreement and wager, a declaration of all that has occurred, but you do the same things that you promised when you were drunk. Affirm to them in measured fashion in sobriety and say: 'Men of Samun, I have promised to drink all the water of the sea, but as you know many rivers and streams run into it to my disadvantage. Keep the rivers from running into the sea and I will do what I promised. And in this manner you will get free," said Aesop. The philosopher, knowing that this was a very profitable stratagem, was very happy. A little later the scholar came who had made the wager, and with him were some senators of the city to require Xanthus to comply with his wager or give up his house. Having heard this, the philosopher ordered the furniture and table placed on the seashore. When the people had gathered to watch, the philosopher sat down in his chair, ordered a glass washed and brought full of water, and holding it in his hand ordered the one who held the rings as a pledge to explain and propose to the public the terms of the wager. And as he spoke publicly to the male population of Samun, Xanthus made manifest to all how many great and small rivers and streams enter the sea. "Let my adversary close their mouths and I will fulfill the wager and will drink up the sea."

These things having been said, all the company of the town clapped their hands and called out, asking the philosopher to go no further with this. Then the scholar opposed to Xanthus, falling at his feet, said: "Great Master, I know that I am beaten by you. Therefore, I beg that by your own free will and moderation the wager be dissolved and annulled." To which by the request of the whole town the philosopher agreed. Thus by Aesop's advice he was freed of the error into which he had fallen.

Afterward as they were returning to the house, Aesop asked, like one who had well deserved it, that Xanthus should be good enough to set him free. And Xanthus, cursing, said to him: "Go away from here, enchanter, since you will not get that from me today. Go to the door, and if you see two crows, tell me, for it is a good augury to see two crows, but if you see one it is a bad sign." Going out of the house, Aesop saw two crows sitting in a tree, and he went and told it to his master. But the philosopher, going out of the house, saw but one crow because the other had already flown away, and he said to Aesop: "Tell me, hangdog, where are the two crows you saw?" Aesop replied: "One flew away while I returned to tell you about it." Xanthus said: "You have a custom, old man, to mock me always with your tricks and caviling, but you will finally have the reward of your deceit." And he ordered him to be stripped and beaten without measure. While they were beating Aesop, a boy from the house came to call Xanthus to dinner. Then Aesop said: "Woe is me, wretch that I am above all men. I who saw two crows am cruelly beaten, and Xanthus who saw one is invited to delights and pleasures. There is no one to whom good auguries are more contrary than to me." Considering these words and his sharp intelligence, Xanthus said to those who were whipping Aesop: "Now desist from beating him and bad cess to him!"

After some days Xanthus said to Aesop: "Get a lunch ready, and let it be elegant and of good quality with a good sauce." Aesop bought the necessary things and coming to the house found the mistress sleeping in the room within. To her he said: "My lady, be careful not to let the dog eat what I am placing here." She replied: "Don't worry, for I have eyes in my backside." And as Aesop was making the necessary preparations he came back into the room and found her asleep with her backside toward the table. He remembered what she had said a little while before, and he pulled her skirts up to her backside and left her to sleep with her uncovered buttocks toward the table. The philosopher, entering the house, saw the woman sleeping naked from the waist down and with great shame called Aesop in the presence of the scholars who were there, saying: "What is this, dirty man?" He replied: "My lord, while I was preparing the meal in the kitchen as was proper, I asked my lady to watch out lest the dog should eat what was placed on the table. And my lady said: 'Don't worry, for I have eyes in my backside.' And finding her sleeping, as you see, I quietly uncovered those parts so that the eyes she has in them would be able to view the prepared table." Then said the philosopher: "Bad servant, you have done vain things but never have you done worse than now, for you have made lewd sport of me and my wife. Now for the sake of my guests I pardon you, but a time will come when I will have you whipped to death."

After a few days Xanthus invited the philosophers and rhetoricians. And he said to Aesop: "Stand at the door and don't let in any fool or illiterate, but only philosophers and rhetoricians." Standing at the door, Aesop saw one of the guests coming who told him to open the door. Aesop said to him some words the guest did not hear. The guest, thinking Aesop had called him a dog or some other insulting words, was angered and turned away, as did many other guests. Finally there came a fairly intelligent man and one not discourteous. Aesop said many insulting words to him, and he, thoroughly angry, answered him sharply. This man Aesop introduced into the house. A little while after this Aesop went to his master and said to him: "With the exception of this man no philosopher has come." For this reason Xanthus, feeling himself scorned by the others, was greatly annoyed. But another day, one of those who had not gotten into the house, meeting the philosopher Xanthus, said to him: "How you failed us yesterday, for the man who guarded the door insulted all of us and called us dogs." Having heard these words, and disturbed on account of them, Xanthus said to himself: "Either I am raving and mixed up or they are." And having called Aesop he said to him: "And what was this about, good lad? It is said that those you were to have received with honor and reverence you mistreated with nasty words."

And Aesop replied: "Woe is me, you told me to receive in the house only those who were learned and literate." Then Xanthus said: "Rascal, do these persons look like learned men and literate?" And Aesop replied: "Certainly they do not look to me like learned men. I spoke a word to them and they did not understand what was said. How can any one of them be learned and literate? But he who understood it well and appeared to be learned, I straightway received into the house." And these words having been said by Aesop, they all approved them.

But after many days Xanthus went with Aesop to the burial place of the great, and among them Xanthus read the letters of the epitaph on a tomb. On a coffin which was near the statue to which one went up by steps, Aesop saw some unpronounceable letters painted in spots and others sculpted as follows: A,G,Q,F,I,T,A. He asked his master what those letters meant. Then Xanthus diligently and thinking slowly and carefully upon the matter and not understanding what they meant, said to Aesop: "Help me to understand what those letters mean." Aesop said: "If I show you treasure here, what boon will you grant me?" His master replied: "You are faithful and of good heart, therefore you will have your freedom and half the treasure." Then Aesop, climbing up four steps of the column and digging there, found gold which he then gave to his lord and said, "I beg you, my Lord, to keep your promise to me." Xanthus replied: "I will do nothing for you if you do not show me what you have found there, for this I value more than the gold." Aesop said: "He who kept his treasure here without doubt sealed it like a philosopher and indicated it with the seven seals and signs printed here, that is to say, with the seven aforesaid letters which mean in Latin: *Ascende, gradus, quattuor, fodias, invenies, thesaurum, auri.* In Romance this means: 'Climb four steps and you will find the treasure of gold.'" And Xanthus said: "Since you are so smart you will not obtain your liberty." Aesop replied: "Watch and be silent, for this treasure belongs to the king." Xanthus said: "How do you know that?" "I know it because of the following letters which are: T,R,D,Q,I,T,A, meaning in Latin: *Tradito regi Dionisio: que invenisti thesaurum auri,* which seven words mean in Romance: 'Give to King Dionysius the treasure of gold that you found.'" The philosopher, hearing that the treasure belonged to the king, said to Aesop: "Take half the treasure and do not say a word to anyone." Aesop replied: "You are not giving it to me, but he who guards the treasure here does so." Xanthus said: "How is that?" Aesop replied: "The following letters show this: E,D,Q,I,T,A meaning in Latin *Euntes dividite quem invenistis thesaurum auri.* Which means: Passersby, divide the golden treasure that you found." Then Xanthus said: "Let's go home and divide the treasure."

When they reached the house the philosopher, afraid that it might be discovered, ordered Aesop put in prison. Then Aesop said: "Weep for the promises of philosophers who, instead of making me free and doing me honor, now put me in prison." The philosopher, hearing these words, changed his mind and had Aesop let out of prison. And Xanthus said to Aesop: "If you want to be free, hold your tongue and don't accuse me so openly from now on." Aesop replied: "Do as you like. Whether you like it or not, you will set me free."

At this time a very marvelous thing occurred in Samun, for while they were conducting public games a single eagle, in a sudden swoop, stole the

ring of the judge and chief inquisitor from the theater or place where the
spectacles are performed, and he let that ring fall onto the bosom of a slave.
For this marvel the company that was present in the theater, murmuring
and relating tales, was upset, worried, and preoccupied. And the public,
gathering together in a council, asked Xanthus's advice. As he was an
important public man, he should tell them what all this meant. Xanthus,
who was very ignorant of the matter, asked for a few days before answering
and went home. Not knowing how to reply or advise the public, he was
thoughtful, meditative, and sad at heart. Aesop came to him and said: "Why
are you so anxious and why is your heart so full? Leave off this sadness and
put upon me the charge of answering this question and of giving advice.
Tomorrow you will go to the council and speak to the people as follows:
'Men of Samun, I am not a soothsayer nor diviner nor seer, nor even an
interpreter-declarer of signs and marvels. But I have at home a slave who
says that he knows about these things and is acquainted with them. If it
would please you to have him brought here, he will declare to you the
meaning of this augury.' Then if what I say and advise pleases the public,
you will have the glory and the gratitude. If I do not satisfy them, you will
bear no infamy; the blame will be mine."

Relying on Aesop's advice, the philosopher next day got up early and
went to the theater and the square where the people were gathered for this
purpose. Going up to a rostrum, Xanthus spoke, and said to the crowd just
what his servant Aesop had advised. And having heard his words, the whole
people asked with great affection for Aesop to be summoned. When he came
before them and they saw his bad appearance and ugliness, they despised

him and scorned him and made sport of him, saying, "What more evil omen could there be than your face? We cannot believe we can hear any good thing from anyone so dirty and stinking!" And Aesop, being scorned by these and other words of similar nature, climbed up into the highest place and made a sign to the people to be silent and hear him. When they were silent, Aesop spoke as follows: "Men of Samun, why do you make fun of my appearance. One should look not only at the face of a man, but at his heart. There certainly, beneath the appearance and the form of a man, learning is hidden, just as with bottles and wineskins one does not look at the appearance but at what wine they contain, and by their taste one judges them good or bad. Thus not only the face but the will of a man ought to be considered." The public, hearing these words, said to Aesop: "If in any way you can help public affairs with advice, we beg you to do so."

Then Aesop with the greatest confidence, said: "Nature, from which all things proceed, set up today a great struggle between slave and master. In this, if one conquers, he will not receive an equal reward, for if the master is victorious in the battle he will obtain glory and gratitude from you. But even if I win and declare the marvel, he will not free me, as he should rightly do, but rather will curse me and throw me into prison. And if it shall please you, make this battle and contest equal, that I should be made free so that I will speak with great confidence and open up and declare what this augury signifies." Then all the company together said that it was a reasonable thing and a fair demand that this should make him free and without bond. And as the philosopher did not wish to do so, the judge by public authority said: "If you do not then obey the public, I will free him in the house of Juno by Pretorian right. And I will give you another in his place." Hearing this, the philosopher's friends warned and begged him to free Aesop from his power and give him to the public. Then the philosopher, though unwillingly, said before the public: "Aesop, be free and without bond." Then the town crier publicly and loudly said: "Xanthus the philosopher makes free and bondfree Aesop, his slave, in which he fulfilled what Aesop said a little while ago to his master: 'Whether you like it or not, you will set me free.'" And thus was Aesop made free and without bond by means of the multitude.

He made a sign for silence with his hand and said humbly and with joy the following words: "Men of Samun, what the eagle is among birds, so are kings among men. He snatched the ring from the hand of the judge and inquisitor, and certainly this signifies that some king wishes to proceed against you and take away your liberty and freedom and to abrogate and deprive you of your laws and thus subjugate you to his power." Hearing these things, the people were frightened. And so in a little while the secretary came with the letters of the king requested by the judges and justices of Samun. And thus were the letters to the senate and council of Samun presented by him in this manner and form: "King Croesus of the Lydians to the senate and people of Samun sends his greetings. I order you henceforth to pay me taxes, tribute, and assessments, and if you do not obey my command as you ought, I will visit upon you such poverty as you will not be able to withstand." These letters thus read and made known in the council, everyone was inclined to obey the king out of fear. But they decided first to hear what Aesop would advise, and he, summoned to the senate and questioned, said: "Men of Samun, even though I see that you are inclined to give tribute and taxes to the king, I do not advise you to do so. I wish quickly to show you what is fitting for your republic, so that you may take counsel about this.

"Fortune has shown mortal men two pathways in this life. The one is liberty, whose beginning is rough and hard to bear. But its end is level and light to bear. The other is servitude, whose beginning is light and level as a field, but whose end is very rough, nor can anyone proceed along it without suffering. I tell you this so that you may think about it."

The public heard these things and knew they were beneficial to the public weal. With one voice they approved the decision of Aesop and said: "As we are free, we do not wish to serve." And they sent the messenger to the king with that answer.

King Croesus, knowing all this and moved in his heart, determined to send to those of Samun, as in his other tributaries, the amounts and copies of the tribute. He held back for the time being, however, because the messenger who had gone there urged him not to, saying as follows: "You will never be able to subjugate Samun if you do not first get rid of Aesop, on whose advice they act. But you can demand through your messengers that they send Aesop to you and say that you will be very grateful and will remove the tribute. And if they do this, then they are in your hands." Then by this advice the king sent to Samun one of his powerful men. And when the messenger arrived at Samun, he presented his mission in the council and persuaded the senate to send Aesop to the king.

Aesop called to the council, and realizing the king's purpose, said: "Men of Samun, I certainly desire to go to the feet of the king to kiss his hand, but first I want to tell you a fable. In the times when brute animals gathered together, the wolves started a war against the sheep, and the sheep, not knowing how to defend themselves, asked the help of the dogs, who warred against the wolves and forced them to flee. Then the wolves, knowing they were weaker than the dogs and they could be injured by them, sent messengers to the sheep saying that they wanted a lasting peace with them but on one condition: that, to remove all suspicion of war, the dogs should be placed in the power of the wolves. And the foolish sheep, believing the wolves, made peace and concord with them under the conditions the wolves had laid down. And the wolves, when they had the sheep in their power and the dogs under guard, killed the sheep. And so without difficulty they destroyed the sheep."

Aesop did not obey the command of Samun, but in concert with the

messenger he sailed away and presented himself before the king. And when
the king saw Aesop, he said angrily: "How is this that the men of Samun do
not obey my commandments?" Then Aesop spoke as follows: "Oh great king
of all kings, I am certainly not constrained or forced by any power or
necessity, but of my own free will have come in respect, and I trust that you
will listen to me with pious ears." And he was ordered by the king to speak in
safety, so he spoke and pronounced in this fashion: "A poor man going
fishing for lobsters captured and caught a locust, which, seeing that his
captor wished to kill him, said, 'You should not wish to kill me, blameless as
I am, for I do no harm to the ears of wheat, nor interfere with the fruits and
grain, but striking with my wings and beak I make sweet harmony and
sweet singing with which I delight wayfarers and take away their troubles.
In me you will find nothing but my voice.' Hearing this, the hunter let the
locust go. And I, My Lord, beg that you not send me to be killed, for I am a
thing of little value and without blame, wherefore I neither can nor wish by
the weakness of my body to injure anyone. But I say things that can be
profitable to mortal men."

Then the king, moved by mercy and marveling, said to Aesop: "I do not
give you life, but fortune gives it to you. If you want anything, ask and truly
it will be granted to you." Aesop said: "I only ask one thing of your majesty,
that those of Samun, who made me free and without bond, be free and
exempted from tribute." Then the king ordered that they should be freed and
exempted, for which Aesop, humbling himself on the ground, gave thanks to
the king. Then, he wrote his fables, which up to these very times are popular,

and presented them to the king. Afterwards, with the letters which the king sent with him concerning the exemption from tribute, and with many presents which the king sent with him, he sailed away to the city of Samun, where the people all received Aesop with great honor. The senate, followed by all the people, came out to receive him, and the city was bedecked and ornamented and made bright with garlands and dances. And Aesop, having been brought to the seat of government, read the letters of the king telling the people and the senate that they were free and that the tribute was forgiven and remitted.

After this, leaving Samun, Aesop went through many and various nations teaching and telling fables and profitable doctrines to men. When he reached Babylon, he taught his wisdom, and thereafter he was held in great esteem and honor by King Licurus, king of Babylon. In those days the kings sent each other letters as a game, in this way: the one who could not interpret a question paid tribute to the one who sent it. Wherefore, since Aesop interpreted allegories and other questions very well, he enhanced the king of Babylon and made him illustrious, and for King Licurus he created questions to send to other kings and, as they were not able to reply, many kings owed tribute to the king of Babylon, by which means the kingdom of Babylon augmented its territory and was much glorified and honored.

But as Aesop had no son, he adopted a noble youth whose name was Enus, whom he often took into the presence of the king, and recommended him no less than if he had been his natural son. Before long his son took up with a domestic or servant of Aesop, whom he kept as a wife. Lest on that account Aesop might do him some evil, Enus accused him falsely before the king and showed false letters in the name of Aesop made for another king and sealed with Aesop's usual seal. In these letters Aesop offered to solve the questions and problems. For this King Licurus, believing his signature to be a true one, and moved by great wrath, ordered his knight of the household, Hermipo, to kill Aesop without delay. But Hermipo, who had pity on Aesop, looking about and giving great consideration, thought how he might profit another time by thinking it over, and so he did not have Aesop killed. Rather he placed him secretly in a tomb and kept him alive. But Aesop's stepson Enus inherited his goods.

After a considerable time Nectanabo, king of Egypt, believing Aesop was dead, according to public rumor, sent questions to King Licurus in this manner: "To King Licurus of Babylon, good health! Since I wish to build a tower that will touch neither the heavens nor the earth, send me artisans who can build such a tower and answer the question, and you will receive tribute and taxes for ten years." When King Licurus received this question, he was very much perplexed and thoughtful. He summoned all his learned men to solve the question and ordered them to find a solution. But seeing they could not, the king fell to the ground and groaning spoke as follows:

"Woe to me who have lost the support of my kingdom. Fate threw me into such a predicament that I asked to have Aesop killed." Hermipo, hearing the weeping and lamentation of the king, came to him and said: "Do not torment or kill yourself. I did not have Aesop killed, knowing that you would repent of it sometime. I declare to you that he whom you ordered me to kill still lives among the tombs for fear of your command. I have kept him in a monument." The king, hearing this, with no little joy rose at once and, embracing Hermipo, said: "If you are speaking the truth and Aesop is alive this day, you have given me new life, for certainly if you kept him in it, you saved my kingdom." And he ordered Aesop to be brought straightway before him.

Aesop, who was not clean and was thin and aged by infirmity, presented himself before the king. Turning his head away, the king groaned and ordered him to be washed and changed. And Aesop, thus washed and dressed again, went to the palace and with due reverence explained his cause, how by his adoptive son Enus he had been accused. On hearing this the king ordered Enus to suffer the same penalty he would have suffered if he had killed his father. But Aesop himself pled for him. Finally the king took the letter containing the question and gave it to Aesop to read. And Aesop, looking at it, before he answered the question, said: "Write, king, an answer to this letter in this form: that when winter is over you will then send him someone to build the tower and will answer everything in detail." And so the king sent a messenger to the Egyptians with this reply. Then he ordered that all of Aesop's goods be returned to him, and Aesop was restored to his original dignity. But the king commanded Enus to conduct himself well, and Aesop received him in kindly fashion.

With such counsels and admonishions and great study, Aesop redirected Enus and instructed him, speaking thus: "Son, look and understand my words with diligence and take them to heart, for we all know how to give advice to others but do not know how to give advice to ourselves. Since you are a man, you are subject to human frailties. First, love and serve God; guard your king; as you are a man, have a care for man's concerns. God avenges himself on the unjust. It is evil to do evil willingly and knowingly to another. With a good and pure heart, suffer fortune and adversity. Show yourself cruel to your enemies so that you may not be despised. To your friends be even-tempered and gentle, so that from day to day they may be loving toward you. Wish bad health and a downfall to your enemies so that they may not hinder you. And covet for yourself the good fortune of your friends and their prosperity. Say profitable things to your wife so that she may not covet another man, for certainly womankind is changeable and fickle. If she is not flattered, she will turn quickly toward evil. Remember to guard yourself against a cruel man. The evil man, even though he be prosperous and fortunate, is always petty. Be more ready to listen than to talk. Hold your tongue and talk little while you eat and drink, for during meals a learned man is not heard, but the witty man causes laughter. Have no envy of those whom fortune favors but rather rejoice at their good fortune, for envy holds back the envious man from many things. Take care of your family not only in the manner of a master, but as a doer of good. Be respected by your own, avoid shame and do not depart from reason.

"Do not be ashamed to learn better things every day. Avoid learning your wife's principal secret, for she is ready to increase your infamy. What you earn one day keep for another, for it is better to leave money and goods to your enemies at death than to beg and ask of your friends during your lifetime. Salute and greet with good will those whom you meet, for we see that the dog is an irrational animal who seeks his bread with a wagging tail. It is bad practice to scorn the troubled and wretched; do not cease to learn good things and pursue learning. When you take something from another, return it as quickly as you can so that, on another occasion, he may the more readily lend to you. When you can do good to someone without its hurting you, be not slow about it. Keep the talkative, ill-speaking, and gossipy man far from your company. Commend your words and acts to your quiet friends, but do such things that later you will not repent of having done them. As there will come tribulations and adversities, do not bear them with sad heart but happily and joyfully. Avoid evil and perverse persons and don't try to advise them. Do not follow the wicked customs of the evil. Be hospitable and receive guests and pilgrims so that when you are in strange lands you may find someone who will receive you. A good word is good medicine against the vices of the soul. He is certainly fortunate who possesses and uses well a good friend. There is nothing so well hidden that time will not manifest it and bring it to light."

With these and other words and with many such pieces of advice Aesop sent away Enus, who had falsely accused him, and after a little while, in

despair, Enus threw himself from a lofty tower. Thus, wicked as he was, he ended his unhappy life.

After this, having called together the falconers, Aesop commanded them to bring him the fledgling chicks of the eagles. Having taken them, he accustomed them to eat while moving up and down with their feet tied to bags of leather, in each of which was a child. And thus, as the children raised or lowered the food, the eagles flew up or down following the bait. After this, when the fortunes of winter had passed, Aesop with the permission of King Licurus set out and sailed to Egypt with the certain and firm hope that he would comport himself in such a way that the Egyptians would marvel. But when the Egyptians saw Aesop, they considered him a monster and without knowledge, a fakir and jokester, for they did not realize that in ugly and dull vessels there is sometimes contained a balsam that is the most precious of all liquids, and if sometimes the bottles are not clean, they contain clean wines. So Aesop went to the palace and threw himself at the feet of the king, who in all his majesty received him in kindly fashion. And when he said to him: "Tell me, Aesop, with whom do you compare me and mine?" And Aesop replied: "I compare you to the sun, and your followers to the rays of the sun, for certainly you shine in no other manner than the sun and the solar circle and disk, and your people shine like the rays of the sun that surround it." Then Nectanabo said to him: "What is the kingdom of Licurus like, as compared with ours?" And Aesop smiling said: "In no way is it lower, but much higher. Just as the sun exceeds the moon and astonishes with its splendor, so the kingdom of Licurus exceeds and overwhelms yours." The king, marveling at such prompt and skillful reply, and impressed by Aesop's speaking, said: "Bring me the masters who are to build the tower." Aesop replied: "After one other thing: show me the place where you want it built." Going straightaway out of the city, the king then showed him the place in the country. And Aesop, in the four corners of the appointed place, put the eagles with the money bags fastened to their feet and with the children in them, who held their tongues in one hand and the food in the other. As the children were borne aloft by the eagles, they called out, showing their tongues and saying: "Give us mortar and give us bricks and wood and the things necessary for building." When Nectanabo saw this he said: "Why are there men among you who have wings?" And Aesop replied: "For many reasons, yet you, a man, wish to contend with he who is a demigod?"

Then the king of Egypt said: "I confess myself beaten. But I urge you, Aesop, to answer me this: How is it that the mares I brought from Greece, from hearing the neighing of the horses in Babylon, became pregnant and conceived?" And Aesop asked for a day to reply. Going to his house, he ordered his boys to bring him a cat, and they brought it before Aesop, who caused it to be publicly whipped with a stick. The Egyptians, hearing this, tried to free and defend the cat, but not being able to, went to the king and

told him of this serious incident. Then the king ordered Aesop to come before him, and when Aesop came before the king he asked him: "Why did you act in this fashion, Aesop? Do you not know that we honor God in the person of a cat?" For the Egyptians honored such an idol. Aesop replied: "This cat this night offended Licurus, for he killed a valiant and generous cock who crowed the hours of the night." And the king said: "I did not think that you would lie this way, for it cannot be that in one night that cat should go to Babylon and come back here." Smiling, Aesop said: "The cat went to and returned from Babylon in the same way as the mares who are here get pregnant on hearing the neighing of the horses that are in Babylon." For these words the king praised and commended the learning of Aesop.

But the following day King Nectanabo had all the learned men and men of philosophic science summoned to the city of the sun. Informing them of Aesop's wisdom, he invited them to dine, and Aesop with them. When they were at table, one of them said to Aesop: "I greet you in peace. I am sent by God to talk to you. What do you say to that?" Aesop answered: "God by no means wishes men to learn to lie; since your word says that you fear and honor God but little." Another said: "There is a great temple, one column of which holds up twelve cities, and each city is covered with thirty beams which represent two women." Aesop said: "In Babylon the children can solve this question. For the temple is the roundness of the earth, the column is the year, the twelve cities are the twelve months, the thirty columns are the days thereof, and the two women tell day and night. For the two continuously run after each other." King Nectanabo said to his lords: "It is right for me to send tribute to the king of Babylon."

One of the learned men said: "Let us ask Aesop yet another question: What thing is it that we never see or hear?" And the king said: "I ask you, Aesop, to tell us what thing it is that we never hear or see?" Aesop replied: "Allow me to answer tomorrow." And when he went to his house, he pretended to write a contract and obligation in which Nectanabo confessed to having received as a loan from King Licurus one thousand silver marks, which he obliged himself to repay at a time already past. And the next morning Aesop took that contract and showed it to the king. After reading it the king marveled and said to his powerful men: "You hear and see that I received some money a while ago which King Licurus of Babylon lent to me." They said, "We have never heard or seen such a thing." Then, said Aesop: "If what you say is true, the question is resolved." The king, hearing this, said: "Happy art thou, Licurus, to possess such a man." And so he sent the tribute with Aesop. And he, having returned to Babylon, told King Licurus all that he had done in Egypt and then presented the tribute which the king had sent. And for this King Licurus ordered a gold statue of Aesop raised in public.

After a few days, desiring to see Greece, Aesop asked leave of the king, promising to return and spend the rest of his life in Babylon. And thus traveling through the cities of Greece, showing his wisdom through fables, he earned a great reputation and increased in wisdom. Finally Aesop came to a city called Delphi, which was a much honored city and the chief place of the region. As the people heard him and followed him there was no honor they did not do him. And Aesop said to them: "Men of Delphi, you certainly are like a tree that is brought to the sea. The wood, when it is far from the sea, seems a large object, but when it is near it knows itself to be small, just as I was when I was distant from your city: I thought that you were the most excellent of all, but now, being near you, I know you for the least discreet of all." The people of Delphi, hearing these and similar words, said among themselves: "This fellow is feared and followed in many other towns. If we are not careful, certainly by his fables and stories he will take away and diminish the authority of our city. Therefore let us take counsel concerning this affair." So they agreed to kill Aesop by a trick, claiming that he was evil and sacrilegious. But on account of the people they did not dare to kill him publicly without reason, so they detained Aesop's servant, who had to prepare his affairs for his departure. And they placed secretly within his luggage a golden vessel that came from the temple of the sun. Aesop, not knowing the tricks and treason that had been prepared against him, left that place for another, called Focida, and to that place the men of Delphi followed him and there took him prisoner with great clamor. When Aesop asked them why they detained him, they shouted loudly: "O evil one, O villainous, wicked man. Why did you steal from the Temple of Apollo and the Sun?" This Aesop denied freely, maintaining it with a heavy heart. But the men of Delphi, unpacking his luggage, found in it in the golden goblet, and showed it to everyone with great tumult and noise and resolutely dragged him to prison.

Aesop, not yet knowing their deceit and treason, asked them to let him go his way. And they pressed and constrained him more than ever, and kept him in prison more determinedly. Then Aesop, seeing no way to escape and knowing that they had decided to kill him, groaned and complained of his bad fortune. A friend of his, whose name was Demas, coming into the prison and seeing Aesop wailing, said to him: "Why are you moaning in this fashion, Aesop? Be stout-hearted and have hope and console yourself." But the people of Delphi publicly sentenced him to death as a thief and guilty of sacrilege of the temple. And coming together as one man, they took Aesop out of the prison to throw him over a cliff. Realizing this, Aesop said: "In the days when dumb animals were in agreement, the mouse and the frog made peace and concluded a friendship. The former invited the latter to dinner. And as they were entering a room where there were bread, honey, figs, and other good things to eat, the mouse said to the frog: 'Choose of this food and eat what suits you best, and you will have a better appetite.' After they had pleased themselves with those foods, the frog said to the mouse: 'Since I have had pleasure and joy with you, it is but right that you should see my house and company and should partake of my goods as a friend and brother. But so that you may proceed most surely, tie your foot to mine.' The mouse believed him and so, with their feet tied, the frog jumped into the river and took the mouse with him, swimming. And the mouse, seeing that he was drowning, said loudly: 'By your treachery I am killed. Some among the living must avenge me upon you.' And while they were locked in this struggle, a kite, seeing the mouse in the water, seized both him and the frog and ate them both. And now, without guilt and against justice, I am to die at your hands and am punished. But Babylon and Greece will avenge me upon you who do this evil deed to me."

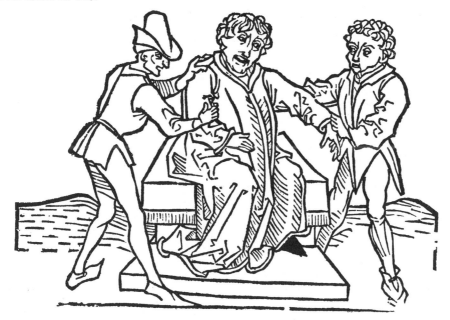

The men of Delphi, hearing this, had no wish to let Aesop go, but rather struggled to carry him to the cliff from which they meant to throw him. But Aesop, struggling, fled from their hands and repaired to the Temple of Apollo and climbed up the altar. But it did him no good, for those of Delphi by force and cruelty took him from there with great wrath, determination, roughness, and beatings and carried him off to throw him over the cliff. Now Aesop, seeing himself thus carried off dishonorably, said to them: "Citizens of Delphi, look upon this your god. Although his dwelling is small, you do not wish to dishonor it, but look with shame and moderation toward Apollo, to whom I had resorted when you dragged me forth." But they, not heeding his words, with great zeal carried him off to death. And Aesop, seeing his end near, said very quickly: "Evil and cruel men, since I cannot make you understand my counsels, at least listen carefully to this story: A woman had a mad virgin for a daughter, and she continually begged the gods to give her daughter some brains. The mother offered this prayer many times and even in public that her mad daughter might recover her mind. And a few days later, being in a village where she had gone with her mother, the daughter went out of the house and saw how a village boy wished to have indecent carnal knowledge of a she-ass. The girl came up to the boy and asked, 'What are you doing, good fellow?' And he replied: 'I am giving some brains to this she-ass.' The mad girl, remembering her mother's words, said: 'Oh, good lad, I wish you would give me some brains also, and if you do so, you will not labor in vain, for my mother will be very grateful to you.' The country boy left the she-ass and violated and corrupted the virgin. And she, thus corrupted and happy, ran to her mother saying: 'Rejoice, mother, for on account of your prayers I have been given brains.' The mother replied: 'And thus the gods have answered my prayers, or what is this?' The daughter answered: 'Just now a boy put a rather long thing with balls hanging below it into my stomach, taking it out and returning it quickly. I received it gladly for certain, and thus he gave me brains, and I feel it so in my heart.' Then said the mother: 'Woe to you, my daughter, rather you have lost the few brains you had.'

"Similarly I urge you to hear another fable in this manner: A farmer, as he was growing old in the country and had never seen a city, and desiring to see one, asked his relatives to take him to the city. They put the old man in a cart pulled by two yoked asses, and they said: 'Now spur them and by themselves they will take you to the city.' But as the old man was going toward the city, a whirlwind came up suddenly so that the sky was dark, and the asses, wandering from the road, took him to a high and dangerous place. The old man, seeing he was in danger of death, called upon Jupiter, saying: 'O Jupiter, how did I offend your temples and majesty that I thus perish miserably? For would that I were dragged and killed or cast down from a cliff by valuable and excellent horses rather than by such vile asses.' And so," said Aesop, "I am not tormented by distinguished and illustrious men, but by useless and perverse servants am I killed."

Reaching the place where he was to be thrown over, he spoke to them again in this way: "A man, being obsessed by love of his daughter, sent his wife to town, and he had the daughter in the house, whom he violated and ravished. The daughter said to him: 'You are doing forbidden and ugly things. I had rather suffer this crime and evil from a hundred others than from you alone.' And so," said Aesop, "wicked and perverse men of Delphi, I would prefer to besiege all of Cicilia and suffer all the perils of the sea rather than die thus wrongly at your hands. I beg you and your gods, and your land, and I admonish all of you to hear me who am dying unjustly that you may receive from them other, more just vengeance in the form of torments and penalties." But, unwilling to hear anything, the men of Delphi had him thrown over a steep cliff, and thus ended the life of the harassed Aesop.

After Aesop's death, pestilence and hunger and a great furor and madness of heart fell upon those of Delphi, concerning which they asked advice of Apollo; and the reply came that they should build an oratory for Aesop to placate and appease the gods. Thus, with compunction and repentance in their hearts for having killed Aesop unjustly, they built a temple to him. By this means the princes of Greece and the important persons and presidents of the provinces heard of Aesop's death. Coming to Delphi and having made diligent inquiry and learned the truth, they summoned to justice and suitably punished those who had caused his death. Thus they avenged Aesop's death. Here concludes the life of Aesop.

I. The First Book of Aesop

PREFACE and PROLOGUE

Here begins the preface and prologue of the first book of Aesop.

Romulus to his son Tiberinus, of the city of Attica, best of greetings, etc. Certainly Aesop, a most distinguished and ingenious Greek, with his fables and examples, teaches men what to guard against in their actions, and because he showed plainly the lives of human beings and their customs, he exhibits and uses in his fables and examples birds, beasts, trees, and cattle that speak as each fable requires, so that men may know the reason and mode and origin of his fables. He told them briefly and openly and proposed true things, both good and bad; he wrote entire passages on the good and he wrote of the falseness of the bad and the arguments of the ill-intentioned. He teaches the ill and the weak to be humble and that soft words are especially to be used by men, and many other things, as will appear in the following fables that I, Romulus, have translated from the Greek into Latin. And if you, son Tiberinus, read them and look at them with full heart, you will find appropriate passages that will move you to laughter and thereby sharpen your intelligence.

Here ends the prologue in prose and begins the declaration
of another prologue in verse.

In order to help and improve the good life, the present book is composed in the manner of comic fables because profitable and necessary things are better and more agreeably received if painted and polished with matter that provokes laughter and pleasure. This garden contains fruit and flowers, and the flowers and the fruit are pleasing. The fruit has taste and the flowers sweetness; the flowers shine brightly. If you prefer the fruit to the flower, pick it, but if you like the flower better than the fruit, take the flower. If you like both, take both. And, so that lassitude and laziness may not make my spirit slumber and my mind defective and lazy, my heart has brought forth a work that keeps it lively and active. And as the prized grain sprouts from the lowly earth, so, O powerful god, may your dew fall upon dry words and may the brevity of these fables bring an honest harvest of customs, as the dry husk sometimes covers a tasty ear.

Here begins the first book of the Fables of Aesop.

Fable 1. Of the Rooster and the Pearl or Jasper

A rooster, looking for something to eat in the dungheap, found a precious stone called a jasper lying in an unworthy place. He spoke thus: "O good thing lying thus in the manure, if some covetous person had found you, with what pleasure he would have received you! And so you might have been returned to your rightful place. But it is for naught that I find you in this place where you lie, for I do not seek you but rather something to eat, and I gain no advantage from you or you from me." Aesop tells this fable for those who read this book and do not understand it, who do not appreciate the value of the daisy and therefore cannot suck out honey from the flower; and to such there is little profit in reading except purely for amusement from these plain words.

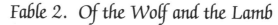

Fable 2. Of the Wolf and the Lamb

Aesop relates this fable concerning the innocent and blameless and the dishonest and evil. The lamb and wolf each for his part came to drink at the river. The wolf drank upstream and the lamb downstream. And the wolf, seeing the lamb, addressed him thus: "Why have you stirred up the water while I am drinking?" The lamb replied patiently: "How can I stir up the water that runs from where you drank before me." The wolf, paying no attention to truth or reason, said: "And for that reason you speak ill of me." The lamb answered: "I did not speak ill of you." Then the wolf, looking at him sideways, said: "Six months ago your father did the same thing to me." And the lamb replied: "Six months ago I was not yet born." Finally the wolf said: "Why have you destroyed my field by grazing in it?" Said the lamb: "Certainly, since I do not yet have teeth to graze, I can have done you no wrong." Finally the wolf said to him: "Although I cannot answer your arguments, I intend to eat you, and after dinner rejoice in you." And seizing the innocent lamb he killed him and ate him. This fable signifies that among the false and evil there is no place for truth or reason nor is anything else effective against them save force alone. And wolves of this sort are found everywhere, seeking an opportunity through tyranny to drink the blood and profit by the zeal of the innocent and poor.

Fable 3. Of the Mouse, the Frog, and the Kite

He who thinks evil and contrary things against others cannot escape, as this fable demonstrates. The mouse, wishing to cross a river, asked the frog for help. The latter was very cordial and said he would be very happy to take him over in safety, all the while thinking to himself that he would kill the mouse by drowning. And he said to him: "In order to pass over more safely, tie your leg to mine." And the mouse, believing his words, allowed his leg to be tied to that of the frog. Reaching the middle of the stream, the frog began to pull the mouse under water to drown the poor creature, and the latter used all his strength to remain above water. While they were thus struggling, a kite came over and swooped down and took in his claws the mouse, which was above the water, and with him the frog, which was fastened to the mouse. And so he tore them to pieces and ate them both. This fable demon-

strates that he who plans evil and harm for others and puts it into practice
sometimes destroys himself in order to harm others. And so perish those
who, under guise of doing good, do evil.

Fable 4. Of the Dog and the Sheep

Of the false men who bring lawsuits and bear false witness against the good,
this fable is told. The dog falsely demanded of the sheep a certain quantity of
bread, which he declared he had lent him. The sheep denied having received
any bread from him. And for this contention they went before the judge.
Before him was placed the dog's demand answered and denied by the sheep.
The dog offered to prove his contention with credible witnesses. And he
contracted with the wolf, the vulture, and the kite to testify in his behalf
contrary to the truth. The wolf, presented as a witness, said that the bread
demanded of the sheep by the dog had been lent to him. The vulture asked:
"Why does the sheep deny the bread he was given as a loan?" The kite said
that the loan had been made in his presence. For this reason the judge
condemned the sheep to repay the bread and pay costs. The sheep, not
having the wherewithal to pay, had to have himself sheared and his wool
removed, although it was winter, and thus paid for the bread he did not owe
and suffered a good deal from the cold of winter. This fable demonstrates
that evil and false men, looking for false individuals like themselves, do
much harm to the innocent and those who have little power to resist.

Fable 5. Of the Dog and the Piece of Meat

Sometimes the greedy man loses what he has by trying to take what belongs to his neighbor. And this the fable shows. A dog, having a piece of meat, was passing over a river, in which he saw the reflection of the meat he was carrying, and the reflected piece looked larger than his own. He opened his mouth to seize the reflection in the water, and thus the piece he had in his mouth fell out and the river carried it away. He was left without the one or the other, losing what he had for what seemed larger but which he could not have. This fable shows that a man should not covet another's goods and abandon his own, which are secure, even though what he covets appears larger. And so according to the common proverb, he who covets all loses all.

Fable 6. Of the Lion, the Cow, the Goat, and the Sheep

The proverb says that a division of goods between the great and the small is never fair, and of this the following is an example. The cow, the goat, and the sheep kept company with the lion, and while they were walking in the woods they caught a deer. They divided it into four parts, and the lion took the first part saying: "As lion I take this part, and the second part is mine because I am stronger than you, and the third, because I run faster than anyone else, and anyone who takes the fourth part I will consider my enemy." And so he took the whole deer for himself. This fable warns that a man should not keep company with those greater than himself, for the lesser do the work and the greater have the profit.

Fable 7. Of the Wicked Thief and the Sun

It is commonly found that evil parents engender and procreate sons who are more wicked and more evil than they themselves. Of this the following story speaks. The neighbors of an evil thief sought a wife for him so that he might have sons. And a learned man happened by and saw that those neighbors wished to please and gratify the thief, and he began to talk to them, telling them to listen to a story. Once upon a time, the sun wished to take a wife and marry her. Many persons, feeling aggrieved, wished to prevent and put a stop to this plan. They went to Jupiter, telling him that the sun should not marry, for it would be to the injury and prejudice of them all, and they alleged other reasons that seemed to them might prevent the marriage. Jupiter, moved by them, asked the cause of their prejudice and injury. And one of them rose up before Jupiter and said: "The causes of our injury are these: Now we have but one sun, and he alone, with his summer heat, disturbs and annoys us to such an extent that he burns and weakens us all together. And what would we do and how would we bear it if he should have sons?" This story means that men should not please the evil and perverse who live evilly. Rather, they should cast them from their midst and prevent them from increasing in number.

Fable 8. Of the Wolf and the Crane

Anyone who does good to an evil man may receive evil in return and not good. In this connection, hear this story. While the wolf was eating meat, a bone stuck in his throat and he asked the crane, as she had a long neck, to cure him and thereby free him from danger by removing the bone. He promised in return to give her a great reward. And she, on account of his pleas and promises, removed the bone. This was the wolf saved, and the crane, begging to be paid for her effort, asked him to keep his promise. It is said that the wolf replied: "Oh, ungrateful one, don't you realize that when you had your head in my throat I might have decapitated you if I had wanted to, yet I let you remove it unharmed. Don't you think I did you a great favor in this? And what more do you want on top of that?" This fable demonstrates that doing good to the evil is of no profit, for they never remember the good they have received.

Fable 9. Of the Two Dogs

This fable teaches us to avoid the bland words of evil men. A bitch was on the point of giving birth, and having no place to accomplish it, requested of another that she allow her to use her bed. After a little while, as she was already recovered and strong, the owner of the bed told her that since she had already given birth and was now well and in good enough fettle to be with her offspring, to leave, if you please! But the bitch she had taken in said she did not wish to leave. Then the owner of the bed began to ask for her bed more insistently, threatening her if she did not leave it. And the other, in great anger, said to her: "Why do you trouble me with insults? If you were stronger than I and my company I would give you your bed, but not otherwise." This story advises us that we should not give what is ours to others in exchange for sweet words, for sometimes beneath the honey are bile and bitterness.

Fable 10. Of the Man and the Snake

He who does good and gives help to an evil ingrate should know that from the ungrateful he will receive no good but evil, as this fable proves. In the winter, when there was great cold and much ice, a good man, moved by pity, received a snake into his house and cared for him and fed him during that time. When summer came the snake began to swell and fill with poison, and he turned against the good man. And the man, seeing his ingratitude, said to him: "Go with good fortune from this house." But the snake, instead of mending his ways, turned upon him. This story shows us that evil ingrates are more likely to grow angry with those who have done them good than to reply in kind; for honey they give poison, and for fruit, pain, and for pity, deceit.

Fable 11. Of the Lion and the Ass

Concerning those who laugh at and scorn those they should not, the learned man speaks in this fable. Some men are mean and mocking and scorners of others. Thus they cause and do evil, like the ass who encountered a lion and said to him in mockery: "God save you, brother," and laughed at him. The lion, indignant at his words, said to himself: "God forbid that I should plunge my teeth into useless blood. It's better to let you insult me than to tear you to bits." This fable signifies that we ought to pardon the ignorant, but we ought to resist and defend ourselves from the madmen who would attack those

better than themselves. And the foolish madman should not laugh at noble, learned, and virtuous men, nor try to equal them.

Fable 12. Of the Two Mice

This fable proves that it is better for a man to be safe and poor than to be rich, unhappy, and full of trouble. A mouse who lived in a city, while going on his way, went to visit another mouse, who dwelt in the country. In his little house, the country mouse fed him some of everything he had, that is to say, acorns, beans, and barley, with much good will. A little later the city mouse, returning home, asked the country mouse if he would like to come to the city and take his ease with him. And after many entreaties the country mouse went along. When they reached the city, they entered a fine room in a palace where the city mouse lived. It abounded with all sorts of food. And the city mouse, showing all this to the country mouse, said to him: "Friend, eat and enjoy all these foods that I have in abundance and from which I have some left over every day." While they were thus enjoying and eating the many kinds of food, there came suddenly the butler, who opened the door noisily, at which the mice were terrified, each in his own way. The mouse of the house knew places to hide. The other did not know where to hide but climbed a wall in great fear of death and in great terror prepared to defend himself. When the butler went out and closed the door, the mice returned to their meal and pleasure. Said the city mouse to the country mouse: "How frightened you were, friend, when you fled. Come, let us eat and enjoy ourselves. You see what food and how many delicacies we have. Don't be afraid, for there is no danger to us in this." The country mouse replied: "You who have no terror enjoy all these things you have every day, since you are not afraid. I live in the good country, happy with all things, and nothing disturbs or frightens me. But you are troubled by many things and have no safety. You will be caught in a mouse trap or in some snare or will be eaten by the cat, and besides you are hated by everyone." This fable impugns those who reproach their betters, for there are some delights that are more than their nature requires, and from this lesson we know that they ought to love the profitable life which is given them according to their estate and live more safely in their huts. Poverty cheerfully accepted is better than riches accompanied by much disturbance and great sadness.

Fable 13. Of the Eagle and the Vixen

This fable shows that the powerful should fear those smaller and lower than themselves. The eagle snatched up and took away the young of the vixen in order to feed her own young. The vixen, following the eagle, begged her to give back her young. And the eagle, seeing that she was more powerful and the vixen smaller and lower in status, paid no attention to her but scorned her. The guileful vixen brought fire and straw and, laying the straw around the tree where the eagle and her young were nested set it on fire, so that the smoke and flame rose to the eagle and her offspring, forcing her to move so that her children would not be burned. Then she gave back the vixen's

offspring safe and sound. This fable teaches us that we should not harm lesser ones lest they avenge themselves upon us. For in many ways the lesser one can do harm to the greater, who may even be punished by the flames of divine justice on that account.

Fable 14. Of the Eagle, the Snail, and the Crow

He who is safe can be destroyed by bad advice, as this fable proves. An eagle, grasping a snail in his claws, flew up high with it but could not break it because it drew itself in. While the eagle was in this fix, unable to break the shell, a raven came by and praised him, saying: "Certainly you have hunted good game, but if you do not use ingenuity it will do you no good." Then the eagle, promising her part of his prey, asked her advice. And she advised him in this manner: To fly very high and let her game fall upon some crag and thus break the shell. "And in this manner we will eat and enjoy your game." By this evil advice the snail perished, which by nature was well protected and hidden. This fable shows that many things are accomplished by deceit and prudence and counsel that could not be done by force.

Fable 15. Of the Crow and the Fox

Those who desire praise and rejoice in it repent of it when they see themselves deceived, of which a certain tale is told. A crow took a cheese from a window sill and carried it to the top of a tree. When a fox saw this, desiring the cheese, he began to speak deceitfully as follows: "O most beautiful bird, there is not your equal among all who fly, either in resplendent color or in disposition and elegant form. If you had a clear voice there would not be a single bird superior to you in beauty." And the crow, delighted with this vain praise and wishing to please the fox and display her voice, began to sing. When she opened her mouth, the cheese she had in it fell out. And no sooner did it hit the ground than the fox, eager for the cheese, took it and ate it in her presence forthwith. Then the crow groaned at having been deceived by the vain praise and at her great woe, though did her no good. This fable warns that one should not listen to or believe deceitful words and vain praise, for vain and false glory brings about true trouble and grief.

Fable 16. Of the Lion, the Boar, the Bull, and the Ass

He who has lost his dignity and standing loses confidence and daring and must depart from his usual conduct to keep himself from harm, as this story illustrates. When the lion was ill, old, and weak and already on the point of death, a wild boar came to him in anger, for he had been wounded by him, and struck the lion, thus avenging himself upon him. In a little while there came a bull and wounded the lion cruelly with his horns. Finally, a donkey came to the lion, his enemy, and gave him a couple of kicks in the forehead. At this, the lion with a great sigh spoke as follows: "When I was strong and possessed of all my strength and virtue I was honored and feared, and everyone not only looked up to me but my reputation alone frightened many into being benevolent, and then I did no harm. Many I helped and defended, and now they are all of them against me. When I lost my strength and power, my honor vanished with them." Aesop warns in this fable that those who have high station should be mild and benevolent, for fear lest they fall from their position. And if they have no friends, there will be no one to help them. Instead, all whom they mistreated when they had their dignity will avenge themselves upon them when they see them fallen from it.

Fable 17. Of the Ass and the Lapdog

That no one should stray from his proper status in order to mingle with his betters, the following fable is told. An ass saw how his master patted and delighted in a little lapdog that accompanied him. Seeing this, the ass said to himself: If my master holds this small, filthy animal in such affection and esteem, and if all his company values her, how much more would he love me if I should do him some service. For I am better than she and I am superior to this little bitch for many things, so I will be able to live better and attain greater honor. As the ass was thinking this, he saw his master coming home and entering his house, and he left the stable and ran braying toward him. Shaking his legs and kicking and jumping up, he put his front hooves on his master's shoulders in the way of the little dog and began to lick him. And he oppressed his master with his great weight and soiled his garments with mud and dust. The master, frightened by the ass's frolics and ca-resses, shouted for help. And his family, hearing the cries and clamor, came and beat the ass with sticks and whips, breaking his ribs and legs, and took him to the stable and left him there well tied up. This fable signifies that one should not involve himself in matters that are not proper for him, for what nature does not give or dispose one for, one cannot easily do, and so the simpleton, thinking to please, causes displeasure and ren-ders a disservice.

Fable 18. Of the Lion and the Mouse

If some low creature errs against a greater one, it is proper for him to be pardoned. For it may be that he will serve sometime in the small way he can. Concerning which this fable is told. A lion was sleeping on the edge of a wood. The field mice who were playing came along and one of them by chance jumped over the lion and the latter, waking up, captured him. The mouse, seeing himself caught and in the lion's power, begged him to have mercy, as he had not acted through malice or on purpose but accidentally, and he explained his mistake, knowing that he alone among all of the mice had been disobedient. Therefore he humbly begged the lion's pardon. The lion realized that he could not take vengeance on the mouse, for he was so small a thing that even if he killed him it would be a crime and ignominious and not worthy of praise. Knowing that to have the power to win or yet not win is greater, he let the mouse go without hurting him. The mouse went on his way, giving him many thanks. A few days later the lion was caught in a net and seeing himself thus trapped began to roar and bellow in great pain. When the mouse who had been freed by the lion heard this clamor, he ran and asked what had happened that troubled the lion so grievously. Observing that the lion was caught in a snare, he said to him: "O my lord, take courage, for you need not fear this trap. I remember the favor I received from you and I want to return your kindness." And so he began to break the knots and fastenings and loops by gnawing with his teeth in those places that had to be undone. And so, little by little, he freed the lion from captivity and returned him to liberty. This fable tells us that one should not presume to scorn or hurt lesser persons, for it sometimes happens that the great need the lesser and are served by them because he who is not strong enough to harm the great sometimes can help him.

Fable 19. Of the Kite and Her Mother

He who forever blasphemes petitions in vain when he is in trouble. And that is what this fable is about. A kite, being ill for a long time and despairing of his life, asked his mother tearfully to make pilgrimages and votive offerings for him to restore his health. To this his mother replied, saying: "Son, I will do as you ask, but I am afraid it will be in vain, for you have destroyed all the temples and fouled the altars and did not even spare the sacrifices, and now that you ask for health I do not believe it will be given you." This fable says that when one does much evil and is then in trouble and danger, the saints will not hear him if he does not first undo the evil. For he who offends many in the midst of prosperity will not find friends in the midst of ill fortune, nor will he who blasphemes and befouls altars, however much he prays to the saints.

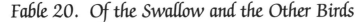

Fable 20. Of the Swallow and the Other Birds

He who does not take good counsel will repent of it, as this fable shows.
When all the birds saw ploughing being done and flax being sown, they
augured nothing from it. But the swallow, perceiving this, called all the
other birds together and told them this was a great misfortune for them.
Afterward, seeing the seed germinate and grow, she told them what would
happen eventually: "This is done to our great harm. Come and let us put an
end to it, for when the flax grows, men will make nets and snares from it and
will capture us by means of the snares they will make from the flax." But the
other birds did not wish to profit by her advice and scorned it. The swallow,
seeing that the others would not take her good advice, went to live by man's
protection in his house, and those who did not accept her good advice
continually fell into his snares and nets to their pain. And this tale is
directed against those who try to govern themselves according to their own
opinions and do not take the good counsel of others. He who fails to do so
takes bad advice, and when he least expects it he will naturally fall into nets
and snares.

Here ends the first book.

II. The Second Book of Aesop

PROLOGUE

Here begins the second book of the fables of Aesop,
the illustrious and clever fabulist.

Each sort of fable is proved against men. For who is good or bad, if not man? It is a great thing to understand the lives of men and their customs, but I have ventured to write similar brief fables, and I shall tell the deeds of the good and the bad, for the former live in safety and have no one to fear. The men of the city of Athens, as they were very good and free men and feared no one, helped each other with a good will. But taking bad advice, they sought for themselves a superior and greater person who could hold back and punish the wicked for their evil ways. Many were frightened, and others who were being castigated as if under correction grieved. Because they received such treatment from others, they were offended. But the more they were burdened by this law, the more they were in grave danger, not because it was severe but because they were not accustomed to being under the law and rule of another. This burden caused them great anguish and, driven to accept it, they wept. To them Aesop told the following fable.

Here ends the prologue and begins the First Fable of the Second Book.

Fable 1. Of Jupiter and the Frogs

The frogs, living freely where they liked in the lagoons and on the river banks, gathered together with great clamor and asked Jupiter to give them a ruler and governor who would correct and punish those among them who went astray. Having heard this petition, Jupiter laughed at them. Yet despite this, they finally began to shout, and as they saw no sign from Jupiter they sent to beg him to respond to their plea. And he, as he was kindly and saw their simplicity, sent to the lagoon a great log. The frogs,

hearing the great splash in the water made by the heavy log, were frightened and fled. But in a little while one of them raised its head above the water to see what kind of ruler they had. Seeing that it was only a piece of wood, he called to the others, and some of them, filled with dread, gathered to greet their new king. Coming up to him, they realized that it was wood and had no spark of life, so they came closer and climbed on it and trod upon it with their feet. So they begged Jupiter again, saying that the ruler he had given them was a useless thing and not proper for their guidance, and that he should give them one more appropriate. Then Jupiter sent them a stork, who began to eat them one by one. Seeing this cruelty, the frogs called loudly and in weeping, begging Jupiter to save them from the stork, saying they were all dying. To this, Jupiter, sounding from the heights, replied: "You asked me for a king and I did not wish to give you one, and against my will and only because of your great insistence I gave you the log, which you scorned. Then I authorized for you this governor that you have and will have from now on. Since you did not like the good, now you must suffer the evil." This fable means that man does not appreciate the good until he has tasted the bad. And he who has what is fitting for him ought to be content. Therefore, let him not belong to another if he can be his own master.

Fable 2. Of the Doves, the Kite, and the Falcon

This story teaches us that he who entrusts himself to a wicked man, instead of receiving help, reaps harm and perdition from such a defender. The doves, being often frightened and scattered by the kite, in order to be safe from him chose the strong and cruel falcon for their defender and lord, thinking that with his protection they would be unharmed. The falcon, pretending that he did so for punishment and correction, began to eat them one at a time. Then it is said that one of the doves remarked: "Certainly it was easier for us to suffer the demands and persecution of the kite than to have such a defender. For now he kills us and destroys us. It is proper that we suffer all this from him whom we thought would defend us, for we were the cause of our own misfortune." This fable demonstrates that a man ought to conduct his affairs prudently and wisely, looking to what may result, for it is better to suffer a small discomfort than to fall into greater danger in order to be rid of that small danger one has.

Fable 3. Of the Thief and the Dog

This is a fable having to do with cheaters. A thief, going out to steal one night, went into a house in which a dog was barking at the door. To quiet the dog he tossed him a piece of bread. At this the dog asked whether he gave it to him freely or to harm him, and said further: "Where will I live if you kill my lord and all his company and steal and carry away the things in this

house? If you now give me bread to quiet me, will you give it to me afterward and will you have pity on me when you see me dying of hunger? I do not want your bread to silence my tongue and deprive me of my integrity. Rather, I shall bark and awaken my master and his family and make them understand that there are thieves about. For I look not only at my present life but even to the future. Therefore get out of here and I will not give you away." Oh, good dog, who would not take bread in order to preserve his innocence. This fable speaks of those who for a single good meal lose many things. For they ought to look at what is given them and why and learn to control their evil appetite to avoid losing much in exchange for little.

Fable 4. Of the Sow and the Wolf

This story shows that a man should not believe evil. A sow in the pain of labor was groaning. A wolf came to her and greeting her said: "Give birth in safety to your offspring because, for the friendship I bear you, it is my wish to serve you in this your time of need in the office of midwife, and I want to give you as much solace and pleasure as I can." The sow, seeing the evil wolf, did not believe his words, nor did she want his service. She asked him instead to leave her so that she might give birth without shame, telling him that he was obliged to do her that honor because she had been like a mother to him. And so the wolf, at her request, left her and she gave birth in peace and safety. If she had believed him she would have given birth miserably, for the wolf would have eaten her and her piglets. This fable tells us that we should

not believe everything that is said, for he who believes smooth and carefully prepared words often finds himself cheated.

Fable 5. Of the Earth Which Was About to Give Birth

It happens that frequently some action or rumor causes fear and terror that is in fact nothing to fear and of little importance, as this tale plainly shows.

It is said that the earth groaned mightily, saying it was about to give birth. And all the nations hearing this were frightened, and everyone was terrified by the great groans the earth uttered. So they agreed to make great openings in many parts of the earth through which it might give birth. Finally the earth was delivered of a mouse, and the news of this went everywhere. Hearing this very small, unpretentious thing, those who had been frightened took heart, and their fear turned into laughter and ridicule. This means that men who brag and make great threats accomplish little, and thus it happens that a small thing sometimes produces great fear and terror.

Fable 6. Of the Lamb and the Wolf

Parents and not birth create goodness, concerning which you will hear the following fable. As a lamb was grazing among the goats, the wolf said to him: "Those with whom you are grazing are not your mother." And he pointed to the sheep some distance away. The lamb replied: "I am not seeking the one who conceived me and bore me, but I regard this she-goat as my mother, for she raised me and gave me suck rather than give milk to her own offspring." "On the contrary," said the wolf, "the mother who bore you is more certain and safer, and therefore you ought to go to her." "It is as you say," said the lamb. "But my true mother, by her own instinct and her desire for my safety, commended me to the she-goat with whom I am living, for among herds and animals the offspring do not get the best of the butchers and shepherds, for each day they milk them, shear them, and kill them for their own purposes. It seems to me that the safest life for me is to live among these goats. "And so he went along happily, saying: "For I wish to live here and will be better off than in the place you have pointed to." This fable signifies that nothing is better than good counsel and nothing worse than bad. And it is better to live away from one's parents in safety than among one's parents with trouble and strife.

Fable 7. Of the Old Dog and His Master

An old person should not be scorned or cast out, for he was once young, and he who wishes to be old should love the old. If he does not love the old he ought at least to love the good deeds of their youth, as this fable demonstrates. A dog had served his master diligently in his youth and early years, in hunting and in every other way that he could. Being now old in days and become sluggish and heavy and toothless, he caught a rabbit in his mouth, but after he had taken it, he dropped it and it escaped unharmed and thus wearied the dog in the field. For this reason the master was angry at the dog. He said: "You used to be good and now you are worth nothing." To this it is said the dog replied: "I am now old and without strength and my teeth are no good. In my day I was strong, and then you praised me for what I was. Now you complain of me for what I am unable to do. Remember what I once did, as I now do what I can, and so I will find kindness and good in you." This fable clearly shows that he who was worthy and did great deeds in his youth ought not to be scorned in his old age for what he can no longer do.

Fable 8. Of the Hares and the Frogs

The following story warns us that evil times must be tolerated, and that while they last men should give way and in order to endure them better ought to look at the evil suffered by others. Because a great many hunting dogs and other dogs hunted for hares and killed them each day, the hares agreed in their counsel that it would be better to destroy themselves rather than to suffer such evils continually. And so, intending to kill themselves by drowning, they arrived at a river bank. The frogs saw the company of hares coming toward them and, because of their great fear of the hares, jumped into the river. When the hares saw this, one of them said: "Sisters, let us not despair. Let us live our lives according to our nature, for there are others who suffer fears and terrors just as we do, and if any adversity comes to us let us suffer it patiently and with hope, for the evil will not last forever."

Fable 9. Of the Wolf and the Kid

It is profitable and praiseworthy for sons to hear the commandments of their fathers, as this story tells us. A she-goat having given birth and wishing to

find pasture, warned her little kid to stay at home and not to open the door of the stable to anyone, for she knew that many wild animals wandered around looking in the barns. And leaving the kid thus she went out to graze. A short while afterward the wolf came and, imitating the voice of the mother nanny goat, knocked at the door asking for it to be opened. The kid, looking out through an opening in the barn, replied: "I hear the voice of my mother but I know that you are a deceitful enemy, seeking my blood with the disguised voice of my mother, and since that is the case, go your way in peace for I certainly will not open to you." This shows that he who obeys the commands of his father and mother will live more securely. And on the contrary, he who cares not for the good advice of his parents will end up in danger and evils from which he will not be able to escape.

Fable 10. Of the Poor Man and the Snake

Let everyone who has ever hurt or damaged someone be suspicious, as this story points out. In the house of a poor man a snake was accustomed to come to the table and thereby kept himself alive on crumbs. During this time everything went well with him. But after a while the poor man became angry at the snake and wounded him with a hatchet. Then the poor man became humble once more and realized that through the good luck brought by the snake he had gotten rich before he wounded it. And because this weighed upon him he asked the snake's pardon. But the snake is said to have

replied to the man: "Since I know what disturbs you, I am willing to pardon you. But although my wound has healed, it should not make you trust me completely, for I will return to your good graces only if I forget the hatchet blow." This means that he who harms someone should henceforth be suspicious.

Fable 11. Of the Deer, the Sheep, and the Wolf

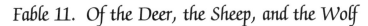

When deceivers demand something through fraud, they bring along evil and lying witnesses, as is shown in this story. A deer asked a sheep for a small measure of wheat, saying that he had borrowed it with a promise to return it on a certain day, now past. This he asked in the presence of the wolf, and the wolf declared it to be true. The sheep knew this was not the truth, but being frightened because of the wolf's presence, asked for a delay in order to obtain the wheat, and this the deer permitted. When the time was up, the deer demanded the wheat, to which it is said the sheep replied: "You strike the ground with your foot but the wolf is gone where he pleases. I promised you what I should not have promised for fear of quarreling with you, since my mortal enemy was present. Great is your deceit but it will not profit you, nor will I pay you what I do not owe you." This fable teaches us that in self-defense we should cheat those who wish to cheat us.

Fable 12. Of the Bald-Headed Man and the Fly

We laugh when someone hurts himself or does himself injury because of some irritating thing done by another, as the story of the bald-headed man and the fly illustrates. A fly stung a bald-headed man every day on his bald head, and the man kept slapping himself on the head to kill the annoying fly. And she, laughing and making fun of him, kept on annoying him. It is said that he spoke to the fly, saying: "Beware, for you are courting death, because although you bite and harm me, I hurt myself only slightly when I slap myself. But if I hit you only once, you will die without mercy." This fable teaches us that you should not seek enmity for pleasure or fun, for, given the unreasonableness and evil of others, you can be injured by the one you hurt and annoy.

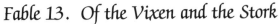

Fable 13. Of the Vixen and the Stork

Treatment you do not want for yourself you should not visit on another. This is to be understood from this story. The vixen invited a stork to dinner and put before her a quantity of thin gruel on a plate. This the stork could not eat with her bill, and so she returned home hungry. A few days later she invited the vixen to come dine with her. Remembering the joke the vixen had played on her, the stork put the food in a glass vessel into which the face and mouth of the vixen would not fit. The stork began to eat of that food, saying how good and tasty it was, and asked the fox to partake of it. When the vixen understood the joke and saw herself mocked, it is said that the stork addressed her as follows: "Friend, if you give me good food to eat, you will receive the same. If you are offended by this joke, you should pardon it, for it is the reward of your own joke. And thus is one joke or insult paid for by another." This fable asks that all who joke in deed and word bear it with patience when a similar joke is played on them.

Fable 14. Of the Wolf and the Statue

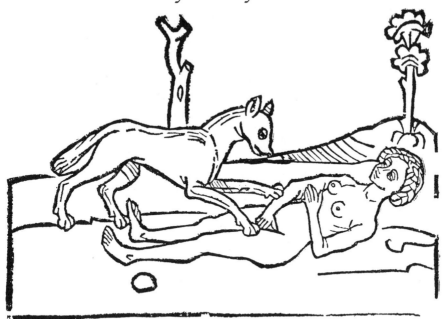

The author tells this story concerning the ignorant. The wolf found a statue lying in a field which he turned over two or three times and said: "Oh, what beauty there is in you, but you have no sense or brains." This tale speaks of those who have beauty and glory and honor and lack prudence or knowledge. And it can well be applied to beautiful women who lack graciousness and can be called living statues.

Fable 15. Of the Crow and the Peacocks

This fable demonstrates that we should not make a show of alien goods. It is better to have one's own belongings well composed so that when one loses what is not one's own, one need not be ashamed. A vainglorious crow, becoming foolishly bold, presumed to deck herself out in some peacock plumes she found, and thus decked out she scorned her equals and joined the company of the peacocks. The latter, knowing she was not one of them, took away her feathers by force and pecked at her. Escaping half dead and seriously wounded, the crow was ashamed. Because she was hurt and torn, she went to her own flock where in her time of pomp she had insulted and scorned her friends. Of this may be said what one of her own kind said to her: "If you had esteemed the garments nature gave you, they would have been sufficient for you, just as your equals are satisfied, and thus you would not

have suffered insult or been driven away by us. It would be better if you had contented yourself with what nature gave you."

Fable 16. Of the Fly and the Mule

Some creatures of little value vent their fury against those who are better than themselves and threaten to do things that are beyond their power, as this story demonstrates. A fly sitting on one of the timbers of a cart said to the mule: "Oh, how lazily you walk. Walk faster. If you don't, I'll sting you on the nape of your neck so that you'll feel it." To this the mule answered: "I'm not afraid of your words. I'm only afraid of the man seated on the saddle who rules me with the brake and even the whip to make me move. Him I fear and not you, for you are foolish and proud to try to annoy those stronger than yourself." This story tells us that sometimes the small and weak threaten those who are better and more valiant than themselves.

Fable 17. Of the Fly and the Ant

Those who praise themselves out of vanity often come to nothing, as this fable shows. The fly and the ant were having an argument as to which was better. And the fly began to reason first, speaking as follows: "You cannot equal me, for I outdo you in all things. Wherever meat is sacrificed I taste it first. I even seat myself on the head of the king. I kiss the ladies and women gently when I feel like it, and in all this you have no part." Said the ant in rebuttal: "You are called an evil pestilence, and you praise your own rudeness with little shame. Perhaps others like you for some of the things you say. You visit kings and chaste matrons and ladies in a shameless manner, and you say everything is yours, for you go wherever you like, but your behavior is injurious and annoying. You grow and prosper in summer, but when the cold and ice come, then you are overtaken and die. But I am happy in the summer, and in the winter I am safe and the weather does me no harm. Many pleasures and joys follow me, but you are chased with a flyswatter and driven out." Thus he who praises himself and speaks ill of others is measured by the same measure and disparaged by others.

Fable 18. Of the Wolf, the Vixen, and the Ape

He who cheats once is always regarded with suspicion. Thereafter, he lives in suspicion, and although he later speaks the truth he is not believed, as one can gather from this tale. The wolf angrily accused the vixen of theft, and she denied it firmly, saying she was without blame. The ape was the judge in the case, and before him were brought the alleged crimes and evils of both. This ape was just and discreet in judging between the parties. He gave his sentence according to what he found in the case, for he saw that the wolf had not lost what he demanded but thought that the vixen had stolen something from him, although the vixen denied it baldly in court. Therefore the ape demanded that the two come to an agreement and that each remain skeptical each of the other, for those who play tricks and do false deeds always live under suspicion.

Fable 19. Of the Ferret and the Man

Sometimes those who serve well are made fun of and cheated, as they do not serve with a good and clean heart. The following fable tells of this. A man caught a ferret together with some mice. Seeing that she could not escape the ferret said: "I beg you to let me go, for many times I have rid your house of annoying mice." To this the man is said to have replied: "You did not do that on my account. If you had done it out of respect and kindness toward me, I would pardon you and let you go, but you killed the mice to eat them and to have meat for your own provision, and my leftovers, which the mice might have eaten, you ate and enjoyed. And the only reason you cleared my house of mice was for your own profit. Thus you served not me but yourself. For that reason I declare that you do not deserve a pardon." This fable signifies that one must consider the intent with which a man does something and not only the deed or act.

Fable 20. Of the Frog and the Bull

If a poor man tries to vie with a powerful one he destroys himself and perishes, as this story demonstrates. A frog, seeing a bull grazing in a pasture, thought to himself that he might become as large as the bull if he could distend his wrinkled skin. And so he began to swell so that it seemed to him that he was huge. He asked his children if he was as large as the bull,

but his children replied that he was not. He swelled up again and asked them again: "Am I as big?" And they answered that he did not yet equal the bull in size. And a third time he tried to swell with great effort until at last he broke his skin, burst, and died. And this says that if you do not swell yourself you will not burst.

Here ends the second book.

III. The Third Book of Aesop

Here begins the third book of Aesop, a very learned man and of distinguished intelligence.

Fable 1. Of the Lion and the Shepherd

This fable proves that the powerful should be kind to poorer and lesser men, and though a long time may pass they should not forget the kindness they receive from them. A lion, wandering in the woods, lost his way and passed through a thorny area, and a thorn got into his paw which became poisoned and infected. Going through the woods with one lame foot, he happened upon a shepherd. As soon as the lion saw him, he began to coax him by wagging his tail and holding up his paw. The shepherd seeing the lion coming toward him strong and frightening, was disturbed by his presence and he gave him meat to eat, but the lion, not wishing to eat but rather seeking medical help, placed his paw on the shepherd's chest. When the shepherd saw the wound on his paw he understood what the lion wanted, and cleverly, with a sharp knife, little by little opened the swelling and removed the thorn and other foreign matter. The lion, feeling himself cured, licked the hand of the shepherd with his tongue and sat at his side, and gradually recovered his strength until he was well. At a later time the lion was captured and placed in the arena of an amphitheatre, a place of arms and battles. Shortly after this the shepherd was taken into custody by the law and was sentenced to be handed over to the wild animals in the same amphitheatre where the lion was being held. When the shepherd was placed in the arena, the lion ran out with great vehemence and fury but reaching the shepherd, he recognized him. He looked around at the great public and roared and howled. Then he sat down with the man in charge of the animals and made signs to show him that he wished to protect the shepherd. Then he returned to the shepherd, for he did not wish to leave him by himself. By this he showed the shepherd that he was on his side, and the shepherd realized that this was the lion from whom he had removed the thorn in the wilderness. When this was noted, both were freed to go where they desired, but the lion wished to stay and protect the shepherd. The public, seeing all this, was astonished and asked why the lion did not devour the man, and when the keeper told the whole story, everyone asked that they be pardoned, and so they were both freed. The lion went off to the forest and the shepherd returned to his lands. This fable shows that one should not be ungrateful for the kindness he has received but when the chance comes ought to return the favor to him from whom he has received a kindness.

Fable 2. Of the Horse and the Lion

Those who know no tricks are at a disadvantage, as this fable teaches. A strong lion saw a horse grazing in the meadow and thought how he might kill him. To get close to the horse in order to kill him, he pretended that he was his friend and even a great physician. So he came up to the horse, accosting him with fine words. But the horse, realizing the lion's deceit, let it be understood that he did not fear the lion, and he showed him a happy countenance, as one would to a doctor. In addition he had thought up a trick of his own. He pretended that he had a thorn in his hoof, and so he raised his hoof and said to the lion: "O lion, brother, I'm glad to see you, for I think you must have been brought here to save me. I beg you to help me, since you are a doctor, and to take this thorn out of my foot, for it is causing me much pain."

And the lion, pretending great sorrow at the horse's misfortune, but with another idea in his mind, came up to remove the thorn from his foot. At this the horse gave him a couple of kicks in the forehead, and the lion fell to the ground with such force that he was for some time unconscious. But when he came to his senses and recovered his strength, he found that the horse was gone. Discovering that his head was wounded, he said to himself: "I have certainly deserved this misfortune, for I came under the guise of kindness and the pretense of being a physician, yet I came to do evil as an enemy." This fable shows us that a man should never present himself falsely and should not pretend to an occupation with which he is not acquainted if he does not wish to fall into shame.

Fable 3. Of the Horse, the Ass, and of Times and Fortunes

Those who find themselves prosperous ought not to harm others for they should know that the wheel of fortune can turn, as this story tells us. A horse, handsome of body, young, and well set up, good-looking and decked out with trappings of gold and silver, met upon a narrow road an ass who came heavily laden from a long journey. Because the ass did not move out of his way rapidly, but slowly because he was tired, the horse said to him: "I ought to have kicked your sides in for not making room for me to pass. You ought even to stand and wait while I pass." The overworked ass, astounded at the horse's pride, remained silent, groaning to himself and complaining to the gods. A little while after this the horse became windbroken from

running and he could not recover, and so he grew thin and no longer mattered to his master, who sent him to another area of his property to carry loads and provide manure for the land and the vineyards. Now the horse, deprived of his gold and silver-decked harness, had to take up the plow and working gear, and thus he tramped the roads and paths. And that very ass, grazing in a field, recognized the horse and abused and insulted him thus: "What good were all the trappings and fancy harness for which you once scorned me with pride and boldness? Now like me you wear the signs of your small-town job. Where now are your pride and your handsome saddle and golden harness, and where is the beauty of your body? Everything you have has been vilely treated and used." This fable teaches us that the powerful in the time their of prosperity should not scorn the poor, so that if they fall they may not be scorned by them. Rather they should do good and be kind to the poor, for anyone may become poor.

Fable 4. Of the Beasts and the Birds

Aesop wrote this fable concerning men of two tongues. He who shows himself harmful and contrary to two parties will be blamed as an ingrate by both sides. The dumb creatures once had a cruel war against the birds and battled them fiercely, and neither side could win. But as they were often in a state of truce, the bat, fearing the hazards of the war and seeing that the beasts were more numerous and larger, went over to them as the conquerors.

Suddenly the eagle arrived to strengthen the birds' side, and so great was the eagle's strength the animals that fled and the birds remained the winners. After that there was peace between them, and they lived at peace as they had done in former times. The bat, who had gone over from his own kind to their enemies, was sentenced by the birds to have all his feathers removed and always to flee from the light and fly at night denuded of feathers. This means that when one deserts his origins and parentage and goes over to the enemy, it is just for him not to enjoy the same freedom as his relatives, for he is not a good citizen who treats with the enemies of his city, and no man can serve two masters.

Fable 5. Of the Nightingale and the Falcon

When a man stirs up ambushes against others, he must fear lest he fall into the same pitfall, as this fable relates. While the falcon was seated in the nest of the nightingale to watch the day dawn, he found the nightingale's fledglings. The nightingale, seeing them in their nest, called to the falcon not to hurt her young. But he replied: "I will obey you if you watch me carefully." The nightingale, still fearing to lose her young, began to watch him, although reluctantly. At this, the falcon replied: "You did not watch well," and he took a fledgling and began to eat it. At the same moment a hunter came and caught the falcon in a snare which he threw quietly and cast him to the ground. So he who sets ambushes and tricks against others, if he is not

careful, falls into snares and traps of the same sort. For if the deceiver, while he is deceiving another, does not guard himself, he deceives himself and others while doing ill.

Fable 6. Of the Vixen and the Wolf

Fortune helps the good and the bad, and those whom she does not favor she disdains and treats ill, and those who hold a grudge in their heart against those who are more fortunate are perverted by this very malice and are twisted, as this fable sums up. The wolf stored in his cave a quantity of meat and provender so he could live in fine style at his pleasure through the long months and days. The vixen, knowing this, came to his cave out of envy and said: "For many days we have not seen you, nor have we walked in company. I have been very sad for this reason. I beg you to console me." The wolf, knowing the grudge the vixen bore in her heart, replied to her: "You do not come here worried about me so much as for a chance to take something from me; therefore, I am not pleased to receive your visit, for I am sure you come here to deceive me." The vixen, sorrowful at these words, went to a shepherd and spoke to him thus: "Do me a favor and I will deliver into your hands today the enemy of your sheep and herd so that from now on you will live in safety." The shepherd answered: "I will appreciate that and reward you." Then the vixen showed him the wolf shut up in his cave, and the shepherd killed him with his lance. Thus the envious vixen got rid of the foreign presence. But later when the vixen was at the mercy of the hunter, she was torn to pieces by the dogs and said to herself: "I did wrong and so I suffer now for the wrong I did to another." Therefore a man should desist from doing evil to a neighbor, so that others may not treat him in the same fashion.

Fable 7. Of the Stag and the Hunter

That men sometimes praise valueless things and scorn good things is shown by this fable. A stag, drinking from a spring, saw in it the reflection of his horns and he began to praise himself greatly, and seeing his thin legs he began to curse them. While he was indulging in these thoughts he heard the voice of the hunter and the barking of the dogs and fled from his enemies. Later as he entered a wild wood the great size of his horns prevented him from moving, and so the hunters caught him. Then, seeing his death imminent, the deer said: "What was useful to me I cursed and held as nothing, and what was not only useless but hurtful I praised." This tells us that we ought to praise the good and useful and not its opposite. For at times what we despise is useful to us and we love and desire what is evil.

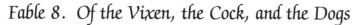

Fable 8. Of the Vixen, the Cock, and the Dogs

It is permissible to undo one trick with another, as this fable tells. A vixen who was hungry came upon some hens who were walking with a cock. At sight of the fox, the hens and cock flew up into a tall tree which the vixen could not climb. Seeing them up in the tree, she began to speak very softly, addressing the cock: "What are you doing perched up there? Perhaps you haven't heard the recent good news for all of us?" The rooster replied: "I don't know what you are talking about." Said the vixen: "The news is such that you will be glad to hear it, and I have come here joyfully to tell it to you. A council general has met in which it has been agreed that there will be permanent peace among all the animals, so that from now on no one of us will live in fear of another and no injury will be done by one to another. For this reason, come down in safety and celebrate this festal day." Knowing the falseness of the vixen, the cock answered: "You certainly bring me good and pleasant news." And the cock, raising his crest and stretching himself, looked in all directions, at which the vixen said: "What are you looking at?" And the cock replied: "I see two dogs running with their mouths open; I think they are coming to tell us of the peace." Then said the fox in fear: "Remain in peace for, but for me it is best to find safety." To which the cock replied: "Why are you thus fleeing, since peace has been confirmed?" And thus was one trick was defeated by another.

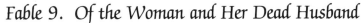

Fable 9. Of the Woman and Her Dead Husband

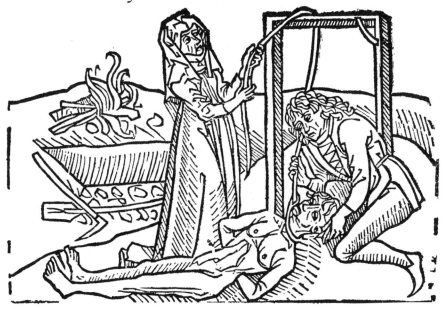

That woman is chaste, in my opinion, who is not conquered by an importunate and persistent suitor, as this fable proves. A woman, when her husband died, went to the tomb where he was buried so as to spend her days in mourning and grief. While she was there, a man committed a crime and evil deed for which he was hanged by the court, and a knight was placed on guard to prevent relatives from removing the body. The knight, being overcome by thirst, went to the tomb where the woman was and begged her to give him some water to assuage his thirst. And because he saw the woman there, he returned to the tomb to see what sort of woman she was. Then, becoming acquainted with her, he began to console her and converse with her, and from there, as the friendship continued, he returned to her many times and to such a degree that one day while they were at the tomb someone stole the body of the gallows victim. The knight, when he returned and did not find the hanged man, fled to the feet of the woman and in great anxiety began to complain to her. She said: "Your misfortune grieves me, but I do not know what I can do about it." The man answered: "I beg you to help me and I ask your advice." Taking pity on him, she disinterred the body of her husband and placed him on the gallows and thus concealed the knight's dereliction with her kindness. And he, seeing her love for him, courted her, and finally she gave in to his request. Although she had been chaste until that time, she committed theft and fornication, one crime on top of another. Thus the dead do not lack those who mourn them and the living those who fear them.

Fable 10. Of the Woman and the Young Lad

Women who are shameless are harmful to men, as this fable tells. A woman who persisted in evil and had deceived many met a man whom she had many times deceived and harmed. He yielded readily to her because of his familiarity with her. And the woman said: "Although many have solicited me and promised to give me many things, yet I love you more than any other." The youth, remembering how many times he had been deceived by her, kindly replied: "I love you more than I love the light of my eyes, not because you are faithful to me, but because you make me happy." And thus by sweet words they deceived each other just as they had deceived other simple people. And even though a woman has deceived you yesterday, she will not fail to deceive you again, and even though she loves the object of her affection, it is not a particular person she loves, for such a woman loves only money.

Fable 11. Of the Father and the Cruel Son

Some believe that the young should be punished while they are young because, when they grow up, it will not be possible to punish them, as this fable demonstrates. A father had an ill-raised and cruel son. Every day he stayed away from home, and on his account the servants were wounded. The master spoke to them in this way: "A farmer tried to yoke a calf with an ox, but by bounding and kicking the calf threw off the yoke and in the process hurt the ox." And the farmer said: "I am not uniting you but yoking you to plow the soil only because I want to break the young ox. For as you injure someone with kicks and sharp horns, with sticks and stones you will be tamed and punished." Thus it is proper for each man to punish his children while they are little, and they should accept teaching from their elders and believe them and do their duty.

Fable 12. Of the Snake and the File

Evil does not make the worse worse, nor does one malevolent thing disturb another, nor should a strong and hard thing struggle with its equal but rather with those who are less so, as appears in this fable. A snake went into

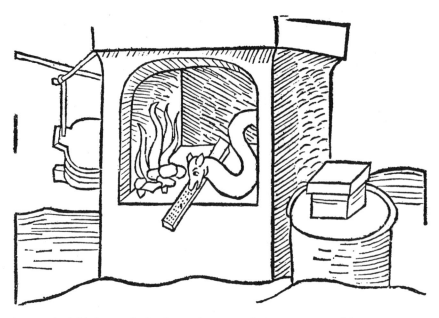

the forge of a blacksmith, looking for something to eat and began to gnaw a file. Seeing this, the file said to the serpent: "What a mistake you are making. Do you want to gnaw and file your teeth? Don't you know that I am the file that files all kinds of iron? Moreover, if anything is rough, I make it smooth and soft, and if I keep on filing, I cut it. Do not try to contend with me. One always gets the worst of it if he struggles with a stronger person."

Fable 13. Of the Wolves, the Sheep, and the Dogs

This fable demonstrates one must not fail to defend the overlord and defender. The sheep and the wolves were waging war against each other, and the conflict dragged on between them, each side carrying on the struggle. Because the sheep were greater in number and the dogs and cattle aided them, it was plain that the sheep had the better of it. Knowing this, the wolves sent messengers to the sheep saying that they wanted peace and concord with them, provided they would place the dogs in their power, and the wolves would entrust their offspring to the sheep; all agreed fully. While the sheep lived at peace, the offspring of the wolves began to howl. The wolves, thinking the sheep were hurting their young, came in from all directions and claimed that the sheep had broken the contract and oath of peace, and for that reason they began to tear them to pieces, for the sheep no longer had anyone to help defend them. And thus we are advised that a man should not put his defense in the hands of his enemies, for this is tantamount to putting himself in their power.

Fable 14. Of the Man and the Trees

He who helps his enemy brings about his own death, as appears from this fable. When the tool called the axe was invented, men asked the trees for a stick or handle for it. The trees said that a very good and durable handle could be made from the wood of the mountain olive tree, and they ordered that it to be given them. When the axe was thus provided with a handle, men began easily to cut great branches and all the trees that they wanted. Seeing this, the oak said to the ash: "We suffer as we should because we gave the wood to our enemy to construct this axe." This fable shows that when a man receives a request from his enemy he should refuse any object that may later cause his own hurt and damage.

Fable 15. Of the Wolf and the Dog

How sweet a thing liberty is is shown by this fable. When a wolf and a dog met in the woods, the wolf asked the dog: "How is it, brother, that you are so fat and sleek?" To this the dog replied: "Because I guard the house against thieves, who cannot enter the house at night because I am there. And if by chance I discover a thief, he gives me a loaf of bread and the master gives me bones, and so does everyone in the house. And they throw me all the leftovers so that I have all the food that I want and I sleep under a roof. Nor do I lack water, so I have an agreeable life." The wolf answered: "Well do I wish, brother, that another such life were available, and that being idle and content like you, I might fill myself with food." To which the dog replied: "If you want to have a good life, come with me. There is nothing to fear." As the wolf and the dog walked along together, the wolf noticed that the dog's neck was wounded and marked by the chain, and he said to him: "Tell me, brother, what yoke do you bear and what thus marks your neck?" The dog replied: "To make me fierce, they tie me up by day, and at night I run loose inside the house and sleep where I like." Hearing these words, the wolf said to the dog: "I can live without the things you praise. But I want to live free with whatever comes to me. I go where I want to go and I have no chain or any other thing to hinder me. All roads are open to me, I can go and come in the woods, I am not afraid of anyone, and I have first taste of the herds and flocks of animals. And since by skill and trickery I know how to deceive the dogs, I live as you are accustomed to do. I shall therefore live well my customary life." There is not gold enough to buy liberty, since it exceeds all the wealth in the world.

Fable 16. Of the Hands, the Feet, and the Belly

He who foolishly leaves his relatives unprotected should know that he thus deceives himself. Nor is anything of value to a man except his own, as appears in this story. The feet and the hands, being jealous, accused the belly, speaking in this fashion: "You alone hold all our gains and enjoy them. To us falls the works, to you the pleasure. While we strive with pain, you eat and swallow with pleasure. So choose one of two things: learn a task with which you can maintain yourself or suffer from cruel hunger." And so they ceased to support him. The stomach, not knowing how to maintain himself, in great humility begged the help of each of them once, twice, and many times, but they refused him for many days, so that, being without food for a long time, the heat of the stomach died and thirst seized the throat, and thus nature fled. The feet and the hands, although too late, seeing that the whole body was going to die and they with it, brought food and edibles in abundance, but they did not profit it because the stomach could not tolerate the food. So the body died and with it the hands and feet and stomach. This fable means that no one is sufficient unto himself, that every man needs relatives and friends, and that we must all work each at own his job, although it may seem to us at first glance that we are working for others, for the profit they derive from it will return to us in a roundabout way. Thus, if we do not work for others, let us at least do it for the good we ourselves shall receive.

Fable 17. Of the Ape and the Vixen

This fable talks about the rich and the poor. The ape begged the vixen, since she had so long a tail and she herself had none, to share a bit of it with her so that her ugly buttocks might be covered by it. For she said the vixen's bushy tail was of no profit to her and was an impediment and burden which dragged along on the ground. To this the vixen is supposed to have said: "Simply so that you may not cover yourself to be more beautiful by receiving something from me, I would rather have a tail so long that it will drag on the ground and through the crags and thorns and in the mud." This fable teaches that the rich and stingy should not keep what they have in excess, since it does not profit them, but should give it to those who need it.

Fable 18. Of the Merchant and the Ass

Many persons, even after death, are troubled and vexed, so no one should desire death, as this fable proves. A merchant hurried along a road with an ass to get to a fair, beating the animal frequently with a whip so that he would carry his load more quickly, and thinking to gain thereby. The ass, seeing himself loaded and whipped while walking far and beyond his strength, reached the point of wishing for death, thinking that after death he would be safer. And so, broken and tired out, he died. But even after his death they made of his hide tambourines, which are always struck and beaten. This means that one should not think that death will mean relief, for one wins repose not by dying but by earning it.

Fable 19. Of the Stag and the Ox

Those who flee are not their own men, but fortune saves them, as appears from this story. A stag, frightened by the hunters, fled to the nearest farm to escape them and entered a stable. He told the ox who was in the stable why he had come there, and the ox answered him in this fashion: "Oh wretched one, why did you want to come here to die. You would be better off in the woods where you can run at your pleasure than here in danger." The stag asked him humbly to hide him, at least until nightfall, for then he would be able to go on his way to safety. Then the ox showed him a dark corner of the stable. And as he was not seen by the shepherds and servants who came in

with straw, leaves, and provisions, the stag was very happy, giving much thanks to the ox who had thus hidden him. At this point the overseer of the farm came and the ox is said to have remarked to the stag: "If this man of a hundred eyes does not see you we may save you, but if he sees you, know that you are dead." These words spoken, the overseer came into the stable, and because the previous day he had seen that some of the oxen were thin because of the stag's eating their food, he began to look in all the mangers. Finding them empty and the hay placed elsewhere, he grew angry at the servants. So he went into the stable to give grass to the oxen and saw the tall antlers of the stag. Whereupon the master called to ask the shepherds where the stag had come from, to which they replied that they did not know. And then he said: "How did he get here?" And they all swore that they knew nothing about it. Thus the master was happy, for either the stag came here on his own or someone brought him. And the stag was there in this way for some days. This fable shows that no fugitive is his own man, but he lives on sufferance like a stranger, and that a master ought to be attentive and careful about such things.

Fable 20. Of the Lion's Deceitful Conversation

This fable shows that it is a torment to speak to tyrants, and to be silent to them is equally painful. The lion, having been made king of the wild beasts, wished like other kings to acquire a good reputation by renouncing his former cruelties. And changing his ways, he swore publicly and solemnly

not to harm any animal, even cattle, but to eat only food without blood. Afterward, since he could not change his eating habits, he was troubled about what he had sworn. So he began to hunt in secret, and to deceive others he asked them if he had bad breath. Those who said no or were silent he took for liars and tore to pieces. Finally he asked the ape whether he had bad breath, to which the ape answered no, but that "previously it smelled good and better than it should have for the altar of the gods." The lion, a little embarrassed by the ape's high praise, pardoned him for the moment, but in a little while he changed his mind and invented a way to deceive him. Pretending he was sick, he sent for the doctors, who took his pulse, saw that there was but little change, and said that because the change in diet caused him some distress he should take some light food for his digestion's sake. The lion—since with kings all things appear legitimate and are praised—said: "The flesh of the ape is something I have never eaten and I would like to try it." Then the ape was brought in for the lion to eat, for though he had spoken well at first, his fine speech did not profit him, so he was killed and eaten. This story tells us that with tyrants it doesn't matter whether one speaks well or remains silent, for without cause or reason they destroy anyone they please.

Here ends the third book of Aesop.

IV. The Fourth Book of Aesop

Here begins the fourth book of Aesop.

Fable 1. Of the Fox and the Grapes

The fox, seeing some bunches of ripe grapes and desiring to eat them, used his imagination and tried all sorts of ways to climb the posts to reach and eat them. But all his thoughts and efforts were in vain and he could not reach them or satisfy his desire. So, turning away in sadness, he spoke as follows: "Those grapes are much too green and sour. Even if I could reach them, I would not eat them, so they are nothing to me." This fable tells us that it is prudent and wise to pretend to have no desire for things that one truly does want when one realizes they are unobtainable.

Fable 2. Of the Old Weasel and the Mouse

This fable shows that every man should learn a trade and an art, for one may be able to do through cleverness what he cannot do by force. The old weasel could no longer chase mice, and so she covered herself with flour and hid in a dark place, hoping without effort to deceive and destroy the mice. An ignorant and worried mouse, thinking this object was some food, came up to her and thus was caught, killed, and eaten by the weasel. And it was the same with another mouse, until as many as three of them had been deceived. Finally there came another mouse, older in days and more cautious, who knew all sorts and manners of tricks, such as rat traps and caves and snares and snakes and other sorts of cheats. Knowing the skills and strategems of the enemy, it is said that he spoke thus to the weasel: "You lure in ignorant and innocent mice and you eat and swallow them, but by no scheme you can invent will you take me, who know all the tricks."

Fable 3. Of the Wolf and the Herdsman

He who uses mild words and is unfaithful and a traitor sins in his heart, as will be recognized in this story. The wolf was fleeing from a huntsman who was following him, but a shepherd saw where he was hidden. This filled the wolf with terror, and he beseeched the shepherd by the gods in whom he had his hope that he would not bring about his misfortune and death. And the shepherd promised him that he would be safe, for he would point the hunter in the opposite direction, so that the wolf might depart in peace. Soon

afterward the hunter came looking for the wolf and questioned the shepherd, asking him the whereabouts of the wolf. The shepherd answered: "I saw him come and he passed here on the left side, and there." He said, "It seems to me that you will soon find him." But at the same time he winked his eye and indicated the right-hand side where the wolf was hidden. But as the hunter paid no attention and made his way with difficulty toward the left, the wolf escaped. Then the shepherd said to the wolf: "You seem grateful to me because you escaped." The wolf replied: "Certainly I am grateful to your tongue, but to your deceitful eyes I wish great blindness." This story is told against those who appear good and kind in the fable but are perverse in their deeds, and it accuses persons who speak with forked tongue.

Fable 4. Of Juno, the Peacock, and the Nightingale

That every one should make use of the grace he has is proved by this fable. The peacock came to Juno in great anger and impatience, saying that the nightingale sang beautifully and knew many natural and clever things, while she knew how to do nothing, and when she sang everyone made fun of her. Then to distract and console her, Juno spoke sweetly to her in this fashion: "Your beauty is exceeding, greater than any perfection the nightingale has. There is no bird like you in color and splendor. You shine like the jacinth, and you have double feathers on the neck and around the collar. So you should be content." The peacock said to Juno: "And what are all these things to me when I am surpassed in the matter of voice?" To which Juno

replied: "I think and affirm that by Providence and their will the gods have divided their gifts among all of you. To you is given the greatest splendor and beauty, to the eagle strength and courage, and to the nightingale its song and voice, which foretells things of the future. It is the nature of the crow to caw; the dove has pity on the old. The cry of the crane always foretells the weather, and it stays late in the olive tree, the garden warbler in the chestnut tree. The swallow brightens the morning light. The naked bat flies in the dark. The rooster knows the hours of the night. To each it is sufficient to know what he knows. Therefore do not seek to have what the gods did not give you."

Fable 5. Of the Lobo Cerval* and the Farmers

It is proper to be merciful to pilgrims and strangers and everyone, and we should pardon those who can do but little, for there is no lack of occasion for them to be thankful, as this fable shows. An innocent *lobo cerval* fell into a trap, and the workmen, seeing that he was caught, came after him. Some hit him with sticks and others mocked him. One of them said: "Don't hurt him for he does no harm and is innocent." And on account of his words, many who wanted to strike him with sticks stopped. Others gave him bread, and still

---

*Lobo cerval means jackal. The woodcut reveals a monster composed of several animals, which suggests that in the fifteenth century illustrators did not know what a *lobo cerval* was.

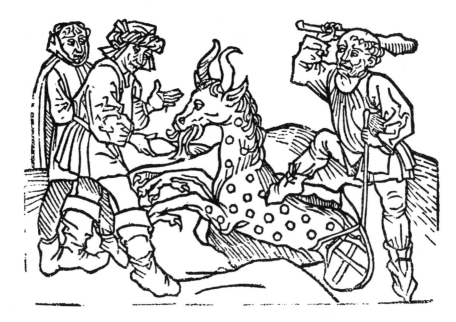

others wept for his spots, according to their diverse dispositions. When night came they all went home thinking that he would not die during the night. In a little while the *lobo cerval* recovered his strength and jumped out of the hole. Free from that danger but with great fear he went to his lair. A few days later, remembering his injury, he went in great anger to the place and plunged into the middle of the herders and cattle and killed and destroyed them. He also jumped on the laborers who were plowing and wounded them and did them much injury. Those who were there saw this and, believing themselves in the same great danger, asked the *lobo* to spare their lives. Then he answered gently, saying that he would hurt no one who had not applied a stick to him or struck him with a stone or done him harm, least of all those who gave him bread and had pity on him. But he would not pardon those who asked for him to be killed but would be their enemy. Let those who do harm in fact and deed attend to this story, so that they may cease to do and speak injury to others.

Fable 6. Of the Sheep and the Butcher

The relatives and friends who are not equal and do not feel that they appear in a bad light are what this story is about. The sheep of a flock, observing that a butcher had come among them, hid their fear and paid no attention to him. Even when they saw the butcher kill one of them, they did not react very greatly but foolishly said: "This is up to you. We will ignore it and you may take whichever one you want." Finally he killed them all, to the last

one. And as he put his hand on that one to kill him, the sheep said to the butcher: "Justly have we been decapitated and cut to pieces, all of us, by you, one by one. In the beginning we did not care to defend ourselves from you, although we could have killed you and tossed you about among us with thrusts of our horns and blows of our heads." This fable says that he who does not look to defend himself and help his neighbor will in time come to suffer and die miserably.

Fable 7. Of the Fowler and the Birds

This fable demonstrates that in no way should we avoid taking counsel from the wise. In the summertime the birds, perched happily in the shade eating leaves, saw a fowler with an evil look working among the canes and reeds with snares at his side. The birds, being simple and ignorant, began to speak as follows: "Oh, what a pious man we see, who, for the great kindness and piety that is in him, has tears in his eyes when he looks at us." And often one of the birds, more artful and clever than the rest, having experienced the skills of the hunters, spoke thus to the others: "Watch out, you simple and ignorant birds. Flee and free yourselves from the deceits of this man, for I warn you that you should immediately fly high in the air. If you wish to know the truth, look at the hunter's works and prudently see which of you he will take either as bites or in mouthfuls, or strangled to put into his sack." This fable means that undoubtedly many can save themselves through the advice of one, and that good advice should never be ignored.

Fable 8. Of the Truthful Man, the Deceitful One, and the Ape

Since ancient times false and evil men have used adulation, and flattery is well received, while honest truth and goodness are customarily pushed away and reproved, as this fable shows us. While two men, one of them false and the other truthful, were traveling through the world as companions, they came to the Land of the Apes, and when the chief of the apes saw them he ordered them detained and brought before him. They were brought before him with all the tribe of the apes present, all making great ceremony and pomp. And the chief ape was seated in a great chair like an emperor, just as he had seen in Rome in another time. He ordered the men questioned as to what was said about him and his tribe and people and whom he resembled. The deceitful and false man began to speak first. He said: "It seems to me that you are a great emperor." But he was asked: "What do you think of those who are behind me?" And the man answered that they were his knights and captains and other officials. For this the ape who was falsely praised by the dishonest man ordered him to be compensated. Having seen all this, the true man said to himself: "This liar who lies in everything is accepted and loved by them and even remunerated, and so much the more will I be if I speak the truth." While he was thinking about this the chief ape asked him: "Tell me who I am and who are these who are with me?" And he who loved the truth and was always accustomed to tell the truth replied: "You and all those with you are apes." Hearing this the king of the apes, moved by great wrath, ordered the true man to be killed and rent asunder by tooth and claw. This is the way of false men who love malice and cheating, for they are more highly reputed in the world than those who are true.

Fable 9. Of the Horse, the Stag, and the Hunter

It is better not to have enmities than later to have them yet be unable to avenge oneself upon them, or to repent and be disturbed, as this fable demonstrates to us. The horse and the stag were enemies. The horse saw that the stag was abler and faster at running and had a beautiful body ornamented with branching horns, The horse, who had been wounded by the stag, went to a hunter and said: "Let me show you a stag that is marvelous to see, and if you can wound him with your spear, you will have abundant and good meat to eat as well as his hide and his bones, and you can sell the horns for a lot of money." The hunter, made enthusiastic by covetousness, said to him: "How can we seize and take this stag?" The horse said: "Ride on me and by my effort you will wound and kill the stag with your lance if you give good blows, and when the hunt is concluded we will rejoice and be happy together." The hunter rode on the horse to where the stag was, and the stag saw the hunter coming and understood his evil intention. With his natural cleverness he ran through the field to the high land and thus escaped. But the horse, when he found himself in a sweat and winded, is reported to have said to the hunter: "I could not accomplish what I wanted to, so dismount and return to your ordinary life." To this the hunter, still astride, answered: "You will now run only as I command. You have a bit in your mouth to stop you from jumping. You are held in by the saddle, and if you begin to kick I have a whip in my hand with which to tame you." This fable speaks against those who seek to do evil to others and sometimes end by doing it to themselves.

Fable 10. Of the Ass and the Lion

Many persons think they will frighten the strong as well as the weak and small with their voice. Of them this fable is told. An ass, going along a mountain, met a lion to whom he said: "Let's climb to the top of the mountain and I will show you how I am feared by many." The lion, laughing at the words of the little ass, answered: "Let's do it." When they reached the top of the mountain, the ass began to bray very loudly, and the rabbits and foxes, hearing his voice, began to flee, so the ass said to the lion: "You see how frightened they are." To which the lion replied: "They may rather be afraid of me and fear your voice in me, for I, knowing you are an ass, cannot fear you." This fable means that anyone is to be laughed at, who can do but little yet who shows by gestures and words that he would do much.

Fable 11. Of the Vulture and the Other Birds

The vulture, pretending he wished to honor the day of his birth, invited the smaller birds to dinner. And when they were in his house he closed the door and began to kill them one by one. This fable signifies that the powerful seldom if ever invite others except to do them harm.

Fable 12. Of the Lion and the Vixens

The lion pretended to be very ill and by this trick got the other animals to visit him as their king, and he continually killed them. The vixens came

before the door of his cave and greeted the lion from outside. The lion asked one of them why they did not come in, and she answered: "I see the footprints of those who go in but not of those who come out." This fable tells us that the evils and dangers others experience should enlighten us so that we may attend to our own safety. A man may easily enter the house of the powerful, but it may be that he will come out late or never.

Fable 13. Of the Sick Ass and the Wolf

The evil man is never to be trusted, as this story shows. The wolf was visiting the sick ass and began to touch his body and asked him where it was that hurt. The ass replied: "The places where you touch me hurt the worst." Evil men, although they pretend by words to do good and help, actually work to do evil and harm.

Fable 14. Of the Big Sheep and the Three Little Ones

Many times the lesser complain of the greater, as this fable shows. Three small sheep, seeing a larger sheep who was running away because he was afraid, made fun of him and whispered about him. To this he replied and said to them: "O silly and ignorant ones, if you knew the reason I flee and am afraid you would not laugh at me." And this shows that sometimes the lesser poorly understand the affairs of the greater, not knowing their causes; if they knew them perhaps they would stop whispering. And so they remain in ignorance.

Fable 15. Of the Man and the Lion

A time of virtue is exemplified by action, as this fable shows. A man and a lion considered the question of which of them was better, and each one tried to prove his ability. As they went along together thus they arrived at a grave on which was painted a picture of a man choking a lion. Seeing this the man showed the picture to the lion as proof of his power. To this the lion replied: "This was painted by a man. If it had been painted by a lion you would not

see the lion choked by a man but the man by the lion." But he said: "I want to show you proven strength," and he took the man to the amphitheater, or place of combat and fighting, and there, struggling with him in actual combat, he showed him that the man is choked by the lion and that the false prowess in the painting did not illustrate a true fact. This fable signifies that a lie, made up of colors, is then conquered by the truth whose power is certain.

Fable 16. Of the Flea and the Camel

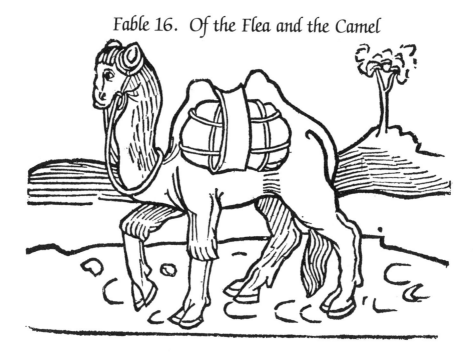

Some folks who are really nothing puff themselves up, as this fable shows. A flea was in the load carried by a camel. Looking at the bearer of the load, he rejoiced, praising himself as better than the camel. At the end of their long day of travel they came to an inn, where the flea descended. Shaking himself in front of the camel's feet, he is said to have remarked: "You did well in letting me down from your back so that I might not bother you or add to your load." To which the camel replied: "I thank the Lord that when you place yourself upon me I am not more heavily laden, nor am I less laden when you get down." Let those who can neither trouble nor cease to trouble the great look to this fable and try to make themselves famous lest they be scorned and regarded as mad.

Fable 17. Of the Ant and the Cricket

In the winter the ant dried in the sun the wheat she had gathered during the summer, and the cricket, coming to her in hunger, asked her to give her a little wheat so that she might not die. To this the ant replied: "Friend, what did you do during the summer?" The cricket answered: "I didn't have time to harvest, for I was going about the hedges singing." The ant, laughing at her and putting wheat away in her house, answered: "If you sang during the summer, dance now in the winter." This fable teaches the lazy man that he should work when he can, for later, when he has no food, he cannot ask it of others for they will laugh at him instead of giving him something.

Fable 18. Of the Sword and the Traveler

The evil man causes the destruction of many, yet he alone perishes, as this fable declares. A man who was walking along found a sword lying in the road, and he asked it who had lost it. The sword answered as follows: "Only one man lost me, yet I caused the loss of many." This fable means that the evil man causes his own destruction, but before he dies he does harm to many.

Fable 19. Of the Raven and the Sheep

Of the injuries done to the innocent, Aesop tells this fable. An idle and lazy raven perched on a sheep and was enjoying herself there. She was accustomed to do this frequently, and so she annoyed the sheep, who addressed her as follows: "If you annoyed the dog the way you do me, you would not be able to suffer his barks or the fury of his mouth." The raven replied to the sheep as follows: "I seat myself on the high hills and I know whom I can annoy and whom not. I am very old, and I am cruel and harsh to the good and humble and a very good friend to the evil and strong, and thus the gods made me." This fable admonishes those who injure and provoke the innocent and good and dare not face those who are evil and stronger than they.

Fable 20. Of the Beech Tree and the Reed

Those who are proud and harsh of heart and do not wish to submit to their master often experience what happened to the beech tree who, when the wind came, did not wish to bend. A reed nearby, seeing the strong wind coming, bent and turned in whatever direction the wind desired. It is said that the beech said to the reed: "Why do you not stand firm like me?" The reed replied: "My strength is not so great as yours." And the beech tree said: "By this you can know that I am stronger than you." But in a little while a great wind came that threw the beech tree down, and the reed said as it bent over: "In this way the proud often destroy themselves by resisting, while the humble escape by giving way and yielding to a greater power."

Here ends the fourth book of the very ingenious and distinguished
fabulist, and there are no more books by him,
but his fables are found in great number.

V. The Fanciful Fables of Aesop

The fanciful fables of Aesop commence in this order.

Fable 1. Of the Mule, the Vixen, and the Wolf

There are many who vaingloriously ask endless questions whose answers they do not know, and they want to become masters without first having been disciples, as this fable relates. The mule was grazing near a wood, and a vixen came to him and asked: "Who are you?" He answered: "I am a beast of burden." The vixen replied: "I did not ask that, but who was your father." The mule replied: "The horse was my grandfather." The vixen spoke again: "I did not ask you that, but what is your name?" To which the mule replied: "I certainly do not know my name, for my father died when I was very young, and so that I should not forget my name he had it written

on my left hoof, and if you wish to know my name, read it on my hoof." The
vixen, understanding the trick, went into the woods to a wolf who was her
enemy, and found him lying in the shade suffering from hunger. The vixen
spoke to him, reviling him and saying: "O crazy, stupid fool for dying of
hunger! Get up and come to a meadow I know where you will find a big, fat,
proud beast. Kill it and stuff yourself on it." The wolf then went to the
field and asked the mule who he was. He replied: "I am a beast of burden." And the wolf asked again: "I did not ask that, but who was your
father?" The mule replied: "The horse was my grandfather." To which the
wolf said: "I did not ask you that, but tell me what your name is." To
which the mule replied: "I do not know my name because my father died
when I was young, but so that I should not forget my name, he had it
written on the bottom of my left hoof. So if you want to know what my
name is, read it on my hoof." The wolf, noting the courtesy of these words
and not understanding the trick, took the mule's hoof and began to clean
it with great care, thinking to find the name there. And while he was
being very attentive to this, the mule gave him a kick with his right foot
in the middle of his forehead which made his eyes and his brains fall on
the ground. The vixen, who was hidden behind a big bush, then said with
great laughter, clapping her paws: "O senseless and brainless fool, you do
not know your letters and yet you tried to read! By my right hand I swear
you have been laid low by a rightful judgment!" Thus do the ignorant when
they try to show themselves learned. Many times they fall into great and
evil dangers.

Fable 2. Of the Boar, the Sheep, and the Wolf

There are a great many persons who are not satisfied with private honors. They yearn to command their betters and their equals, concerning which you will hear a fable as follows: A small boar lived among a great herd of swine. He was proud but indignant because he was not the principal and the greatest and could not command all the swine. He ran around the herd acting ferocious, growling, and sharpening his tusks, thinking to frighten others.

But since he saw that not one of them was frightened, with great wrath he spoke as follows: "What is the advantage of staying here, since in this flock when I give orders no one obeys me, and although I wax wroth no one flees from me? If I threaten, they pay me no attention."

He decided not to stay there any longer and departed and went his chanceful way. Going along he came to a flock of sheep, and when he was in their midst, he ran about grunting and sharpening his teeth. Seeing this, the sheep were terrified and began to flee in every direction. The boar, amazed, said: "It suits me to dwell here and I am due this honor. When I grow angry they all run from me, and if I threaten them, they all are frightened. Here I'll be honored and loved by all."

Matters went in this way for several days, when along came a very hungry wolf who, seeing the sheep, wanted to eat them. When they saw him coming after them, they fled into the hills. But the boar, thinking to defend the sheep, would not flee, and so the wolf seized him and carried him into the forest. And as it happened, they came to the great herd of swine from which the boar had departed. Recognizing them, he began to call for help in a loud voice. When they recognized him, they all rose up together against the wolf and saved their brother, who was wounded almost to the point of death. Then the boar, in their midst and full of grief and shame, said: "Now I know the truth of the proverb saying that in luck, whether adversity or prosperity, it is always good to be with one's relations. For surely if I had not left my relatives, I would not have suffered these misfortunes." And so many men who wish to rule arrogantly beyond their due frequently fall into evils and misfortune.

Fable 3. Of the Fox and the Rooster

Many persons who speak without thinking ahead say things which later they regret, and even evil and harm come of such things. Concerning this is our fable. The fox, being hungry, went to a house, and coming up to a rooster, he said: "O lord rooster, what a wonderful voice your father had. He was very much my lord, and I think you must have the same voice, and so for the great friendship which I had with him I have come to become acquainted with you; for which reason I beg you to sing, as I would like to know whether you have

as fine a voice or an even better one." The rooster, believing these words and answering his request, began to sing with his eyes closed. The fox then jumped upon him and carried him to his den, and the men of the place who heard it followed the fox. Hearing this, the rooster said to the fox: "Do you hear what those rough villagers are saying? Tell them that I am not theirs but yours, and that you are carrying away your rooster and not theirs." So the fox, dropping the rooster from his mouth, said: "I am carrying away my rooster and not yours." And while the fox was speaking the rooster flew up into a tree and answered the fox: "You lie, my lord, boldly. For I am theirs and not yours." The fox, seeing himself deceived, biting his lips and said: "Oh mouth, how many things you say which then are a burden to you! For certainly if you had kept silent now you would not have lost the rooster you hunted down." And this signifies that many men say without thinking things which afterward they may repent having said. And even harm and evil come to them from these things.

Fable 4. Of the Dragon and the Farmer

It happens many times that men return bad for good and harm those who help them, as this fable will show. A dragon lived in a river, and as its waters rose he continued down river. Meanwhile the river dried up, leaving him on a sandbar, and there he lay, unable to move without water. A farmer passed by and said: "O dragon, how do you happen to be here this way?" The dragon replied: "I followed the rising river downstream, and now that the water has gone down, it has left me high and dry in this place, and I cannot move

without water. But if you will bind me to your ass and carry me to my house, you will receive gold and silver and many other good things from me." Then the farmer, led on by his cupidity, tied up the dragon and put him on his ass and carried him and put him in his cave. Lowering him from the ass, the farmer set him at liberty and then asked him to give him what he had promised. Then the dragon said to the countryman: "What? For tying me up, you ask gold and silver?" The rustic said, "You yourself asked me to tie you." To which the dragon answered: "We are not talking about that. But first I want to eat you, for I am hungry." The farmer said: "According to that, you give evil for good."

While they were thus talking, it happened that a vixen came by who heard all those words and said: "Why do you have a discord between you and differ?" the dragon began to speak first and said to her: "This farmer tied me tight, and putting me upon his donkey brought me here, and now he asks me for I don't know what." Then the man said: "Listen, my lady fox. This dragon was carried away by the river and cast upon a sandbar, and as I was passing there he asked me to tie him on my ass and bring him home, promising me gold and silver and many other things. And now he not only won't keep his word, he even wants to eat me." The vixen replied: "You did a foolish thing when you tied him, but show me now how you tied him and then I will render a judgment." Then the farmer began to tie the dragon, and the vixen asked the dragon: "Did he tie you as tightly as that?" And the dragon replied: "Not only that tight, but a hundred times tighter." And the vixen said to the farmer: "Tighten it." The farmer, as he was strong, tightened the ropes and he tied the dragon as tightly as he could. And the vixen asked the dragon:

"Did he tie you that tight?" And the dragon replied, "My lady, he certainly did." The vixen then said to the farmer: "Tie the knot so that it may be very tight and tighten the loops, for he who ties well unties equally well. And put the dragon on the ass again and return to the place where you got him and leave him there tied up as he is, and he won't be able to eat you." The farmer did as the vixen decreed. And those who return good for evil sometimes receive their just reward.

Fable 5. Of the Vixen and the Cat

This parable speaks of men who flatter themselves that they know many things and, thinking themselves subtle and clever, laugh and make fun of many others. The vixen, meeting a cat, greeted him, saying: "Brother, remain safe from the evil ones." The cat answered: "Greetings to you, too." Then the vixen asked the cat what tricks he knew and how many, and the cat said: "I know nothing of tricks, but I know how to jump and climb trees and walls, and in this way I escape from dangers." Then it is said that the vixen spoke thus: "By my head, you do not deserve to live, since you know no more and are ignorant and stupid." The cat answered: "That's what you say. I beg you to show me all the tricks you know." The vixen replied: "I know one hundred tricks, not just in middling fashion but perfectly, each one of them, which enable me to live honorably and to escape from many dangers." The cat, hearing this, said: "Certainly you deserve a long life and lasting health, since you are so wise and learned." And speaking in this manner the cat said to the vixen: "Sister, I see a man on horseback coming with two very large and fast dogs, our enemies." Said the vixen: "You do not know what you are saying. You are ignorant and fearful and that is why you say such things, and even if that were true, why hurry?" When the horse and dogs came closer and the dogs saw the vixen and the cat, they began to run toward them. Then the vixen, seeing the dogs getting close, said to the cat: "Brother, let us flee." The cat replied: "Perhaps we must, but each one for himself." So each of them ran off. The cat, finding a very tall tree, quickly climbed it and thus saved himself. The dogs, leaving the cat, caught the vixen, which was running lazily. And the cat called to her in a loud voice, saying: "Sister, now it is time to use some of those hundred tricks, for now you are far away from the woods." But when the dogs caught the vixen her tricks did her no good, and they killed her. This fable warns the wise, who are studious, clever, and sly, not to mistreat or laugh at the ignorant and weak.

Fable 6. Of the Wolf and the Goat

The sick and poor often rise against the powerful who treat them badly, as this fable relates. A wolf followed the male of a herd of goats in order to capture him. The billy goat went up to the top of a lofty crag where he was safe. The wolf blocked him and hemmed him in from the foot of the crag, but after three or four days, the wolf for hunger and the goat for thirst separated, each going his own way, first the wolf and then the goat. The goat went to the river and drank copiously of the water, and looking at his reflection in the water, said to himself: "Oh, what good legs and what a handsome beard I have and what great horns! And having all these perfections a single wolf makes me flee? From now on I shall wait for him here and stand up to him, and I shall not run away or give him any advantage." The wolf, standing behind him, listened to all this in silence. Then coming up to him he seized the goat by the leg with his teeth and said: "What is this? Why do you talk in this fashion, brother goat?" And the goat, realizing he was caught and in the wolf's power, said: "O my lord wolf, have mercy on me for I know my fault, for a goat after he has drunk speaks in parables and says more than he should." But the wolf paid no attention to the goat's words and ate him up. This story shows us that the small and poor should not rise up against the powerful beyond their strength.

Fable 7. Of the Wolf and the Ass

A man should not lightly take counsel from one he wishes to harm, as this fable proves. The wolf, meeting an ass, said to him: "Brother Ass, I am very desirous of eating, so I have you to eat." The ass replied: "As it pleases you, sir, so be it, for it is your right to command and my duty to obey. And if you eat me you will free me from many burdens, since I carry the wine from the wine press and the wheat from the threshing floor, and the wood from the forest. In addition I carry stones to build houses and the wheat to be milled at the mill, and I bring it back. In sum, I do all that has to be done and all the work is for me. For this reason I often curse the day I was born because of all the work I have to do. But I ask of you only one thing: that you hear me. I ask you not to eat me on this road, because I should be ashamed before the neighbors and on account of my lord, who would say: 'How did this ass happen to let himself be eaten by the wolf?' For this reason take my advice. Let us go to the woods and make nooses, and you can tie me by the neck as if I were your slave, as I am. And you must take me down to the woods and you may eat me there in peace, as you desire." The wolf, who did not understand the trick, said: "Let us do as you say."

And so, going to the woods, they made some very tight loops, the wolf twisting them and the ass binding them and arranging them so that the wolf held the ass by the chest and the ass bound the wolf very tightly by the neck. Then the ass said: "Let us go wherever you wish." The wolf said: "Show the way." The ass replied: "Gladly will I do so." And so the ass began to walk in the direction of his master's house, and the wolf saw the neighborhood and the town and said: "Look, we are not going the right way." And the ass replied: "Sir, do not say that. For if it please you, this is the right road." The wolf, recognizing the trick, began to draw back and the ass pulled strongly toward home and they both arrived at the master's door. Seeing this the master came out of the house with all his company and wounded the wolf almost to the point of death. And one of them, intending to give him a great blow on the head with an axe, missed his aim and cut the rope and thus freed the wolf, who fled to the woods. And the ass entered the house of his master, upset by the fear he had endured. And with great joy, seeing that he had escaped from the wolf's power, he began to bray and make a great noise. When the wolf heard this from the woods, he said, "However much noise you make you will not catch me there." This fable teaches us that we should not lightly believe those to whom we wish to do harm and mischief. And when we were deceived, all the better must we guard ourselves from then on.

Fable 8. Of the Snake and the Farmer

A man should not trust or believe someone he intends to harm, or to whom he has done harm. For he will finally reap harm and evil from him, as this tale describes. A farmer went to sow a field, and passing along a road he cruelly trod upon a snake, which said to him: "Oh evil friend, why have you thus trod upon me without my deserving any harm from you. Look, I tell you not to believe anyone you have harmed." But the farmer went on his way paying little attention to these words. The next year when the same farmer passed along the same path, the snake spoke to him: "Where are you going, friend?" To which the farmer replied: "I am going to sow my field." And the

snake said: "Be careful not to sow on irrigated land, for this year there will be a lot of rain, and what is sown in a wet place will be drowned. But be careful not to believe someone whom you have harmed." And the farmer went away thinking that the snake was speaking falsely. So he sowed on wet and irrigated land. There was much rain that year and the seeds on the wet lands died, and so the man harvested nothing. The following year the farmer was passing along the same road on his way to sow, and the snake asked him: "Where are you going, friend?" And he said he was going to sow. This time she warned him not to sow in a dry place because that year there would be much hot weather and everything sown in a dry place would dry up. Finally she said: "But do not believe someone you have harmed." The farmer, thinking she wished to deceive him, paid no attention to what she said and sowed on dry ground. That year a prolonged hot spell and drought occurred so that the whole countryside dried up and all the dry land was lost. In the third year, when the same farmer was passing the snake, she said to him: "Where are you going, man?" He answered: "I am going to sow my lands." And the snake said: "If you wish to grow wheat this year, sow on the common lands, for they are neither very dry nor very wet, but temperate. But I tell you again, whom you hurt you must not believe." The farmer did that year what the snake advised, and everything came out as the snake had predicted, and he got a great deal of wheat that year.

As the good man was returning from his property, the snake said to him: "Notice, friend, that everything has come out as I said it would." And the farmer replied, "Certainly, things have come out as you first said they would. For this I give you many thanks." The snake then asked him to do her some favor in payment. The farmer asked her: "What reward do you ask of me." The snake said: "I ask no other thing except that tomorrow you send me the only son you have with a jar of milk." And she showed him a hole in which to put the milk. And she added: "Notice that I have often said that him whom you have harmed you should not believe." With this the good man went home and the next morning he sent his son as he had promised. When the son reached the place his father had shown him, he put the milk in the hole. Then the snake, coming out, attacked the boy and bit him so that he died at once. The grieving father came to the snake and spoke to her: "You have deceived me and evilly killed my son." The snake, lying on a high crag, answered him, saying: "I deny what you say, for I did nothing deceitfully, but you wounded me without any reason and without cause, and you never made it up. And I always told you not to believe anyone whom you had harmed." This fable warns us not to believe anyone to whom we have done harm or wrong.

Fable 9. Of the Vixen, the Fisherman, and the Wolf

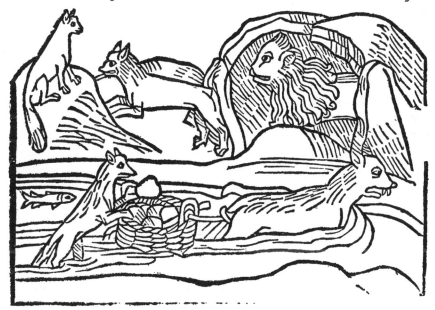

If anyone is injured or harmed, he should not avenge himself with his tongue, by speaking evil, for this is no honest vengeance, as this fable proves. A vixen was eating a fish in the vicinity of a river. A wolf, coming there hungry, asked for part of the food. The vixen replied: "Sir, do not talk to me of that, for it would not be honest or proper for you to eat the leavings of my table. May God never bring you down to such a degree. But I will give you some advice. Bring me a basket, and I will show you the art of fishing, so that when you lack other food at least you will not lack fish, of which you will have plenty." The wolf went to the first town and stole from there a very large basket and brought it to the vixen. And she fastened it very tightly to his tail. She said to him: "Go into the water and walk forward with your tail dragging and I will go behind driving, urging, and moving the fish and thus you will know how to fish as well as you know how to hunt."

The wolf, believing the vixen, went into the river with the basket tied to his tail, and the vixen threw stones in it. And when the basket was full the wolf said: "I cannot move with the basket, as full as it is." The vixen answered: "I thank the Lord that I see you so good a fisherman and well learned in this art. Wait a bit while I look for someone who can help us take out the fish."

Then she went to the town and said to men: "What are you about? Know that the wolf who eats your sheep and lambs and other animals, not content with that, takes the fish out of your river." Hearing this, they all went out with lances and swords and dogs toward the wolf and wounded him almost unto death. And one, planning to deal a great knife blow to end the matter, hit the wolf's tail, cutting it off entirely. And so, as the wolf saw himself free of his burden and without a tail, he fled and so escaped, half dead.

At this time it happened that there was in that province a lion, king of all the animals, who was ill, whom all the beasts went to visit. Among them came that fisherman wolf and said to the lion: "Oh my lord and natural king, I, your servant, have gone about looking for some medicine for your health and I have nothing except that I have learned that there lives in this gluttonous and proud province a vixen who has within herself great medicine. If you wish her to come, summon her to council. Flay her, but so that she remains alive. And wrap your belly and the entrance to your stomach with her hide. Then you will get well." The vixen had her cave not far from where the lion lived on a crag, and she listened most carefully to all these words. As the wolf came away from the lion, she covered herself with mud and came before the lion and said to him: "Lord, save me." And the lion said: "Be saved. But come closer, as I wish to kiss you and tell you a secret." The vixen answered: "You see, Sir, I was so anxious to come and visit you that I'm all muddy and covered with manure. I am ashamed to approach you lest you become annoyed and disgusted. After I have bathed and combed, I will come before my lord the king, and you may say what you will. But before I make my obeisance, I want to tell you why I come in such complaining fashion. I have traveled over almost the entire world, and I have not been able to find out more than what a Greek physician showed me in Athens. In this province they say there is a wolf without a tail who is big and fat, and who lost his tail by similar medicine. The Greek says that this wolf has medicine for your health, so, when you call him before you, extend your beautiful paws toward him and skin him alive. And leave the head and feet to be cut off, for they say that these parts are poisonous, but with his warm skin wrap up your belly, and then you will be well and happy." Having said these words, she left.

A little while later the wolf came to the lion asking for advice. The lion extending his strong paws, did as the vixen had ordered and skinned him except for the skin covering his head and feet. And so with the warm, recently stripped skin he wrapped his belly. And the flies, wasps, and beetles began to attack the wolf and bit him harshly. As he ran from them as fast as he could, the vixen, who was sitting on a lofty crag, called to him with a loud laugh: "Who are you, going about with your hat on your head and gloves on your hands in such warm weather? And while you run through this meadow, listen to what I tell you. When you are at home, speak well of the master, and when you are in court speak well of everybody. If you desire to say neither good nor evil, let it be." This fable teaches that whoever has been injured by someone should not receive the vengeance of words, nor should he speak ill or blaspheme him in public or in private, and he who sets a trap against his brother may himself fall into it.

Fable 10. Of the Wolf Who Farted

Many persons who seek objects higher than are suitable for them and presume further than their status requires, demand what is not proper for them. And usually the higher they rise the greater their fall, as this fable shows.

The wolf rising and stretching one morning let go a sound from behind, and said: "This is a good sign. I thank the gods that today I shall be heaped and showered with honors, as my tail has shown me by farting." And so, setting out on his adventures on the road, he came upon a quantity of salted bacon that had fallen from [the back of] some muleteers, and as he smelled it, he turned from one side to the other and said: "I shall not partake of you today, for you turn my stomach and I am certain that today I am to be filled with honors, as this morning my rear end showed me." Going farther on, he found some dry salt bacon, and turning it over he said: "I will not eat you, for I am certain that today I am to be full of good viands, as my tail told me." And going down into a valley he found there a mare with a colt and said to himself: "God be thanked that I knew that today I am to be loaded down with dignities." Coming up to the mare he said to her: "Sister, I came along the road hungry, so it is proper for you to give me your colt to eat." The mare replied: "As it please you, so let it be done. But when riding me yesterday my master allowed a thorn to get in my foot. I beg you, since you are a doctor and a famed surgeon, to take it out and cure me first, after which we will be at your service and you may command me and shall eat this, my son." The wolf, believing this, approached the mare's foot to remove the thorn, and she gave him a great kick in the middle of his forehead which laid him low. So she sped away with her colt to the mountains and was free of danger. The wolf recovering, and getting back his strength, said to himself: "I care nothing for this injury, for I know that today I shall be filled."

He went on his way until he encountered two sheep quarreling in a meadow. And he said to himself: "Now it is certain. Now I am to be full. To God be thanks." And coming up to the two sheep, he greeted them and said: "Brothers, prepare yourselves, for one of you two will invite me to dinner." One of the sheep answered: "Let it be as you please, but we beg you to judge between us fairly concerning this meadow which belonged to our fathers. Because we do not have knowledge of the matter and have not made use of lawsuits or judgments, we are quarreling about it. Make between us a rightful decision of it and then do with us as you will."

The wolf answered: "I will gladly do that, but I should like you to ask me in what manner you want it divided." Then the other sheep said: "Sir, since you ask, I think you ought to divide it this way: You should stand in the middle of the field and each of us will go to an end of the field and both of us will run to where you are. The one who gets there first will have the meadow and the other you will eat." The wolf said: "Let it be done. It is a good way." So each sheep went his way. And they ran with great zeal and force to where the wolf stood in the middle of the field, and as they reached him at the same time, they hit the wolf a double blow so hard that he fell to the ground, breaking his ribs, and he all but died, dirtying himself with his own excrement. But a little while later, recovering, he said: "I do not even care about this additional injury for I am to be fed today, as my tail told me this morning." Leaving there he encountered on a river bank a sow with her little pigs grazing in a meadow. And he said: "Glory to thee, o Lord! I knew that I was to be filled with delicate viands." And he said to the sow: "Sister, I shall eat your piglets." She answered: "Sir, as you command, but they are not yet washed according to our rite and sect, so I beg of you, since good fortune brought you here, that you act as priest and baptize them according to our law. After that choose among them those that please you most." And the wolf asked that she show him the spring. The sow then showed him a mill stream, saying that this was the sanctified spring. When he was in the midst of the stream, the wolf, acting as priest, taking one of the suckling pigs to put it in the water and wash it according to ceremony, the sow came and gave him a hard blow with her snout, grunting furiously, and threw him into the stream. The force of the water, which was running hard, carried away the wolf so that he fell backwards into the mill wheel, dancing a little, and he suffered a good deal in his body. Escaping from there with great effort, he said to himself that although the pain was very great it would not make him go back on his plan, and that it was really no injury for it had been done to him by a trick. He still understood that, because in the morning his rear had sounded off, he was to be filled on that day with delicate viands.

And so, passing near a town, he saw some goats on top of an oven and said: "Thanks be to God, now I see meat that I so desire," and he went toward them. When they saw the wolf, the goats hid inside the furnace, and the wolf, standing in front of the oven, greeted them, saying: "Sisters, may you have health. I have come to visit you and to eat one of you." And they said: "Sir, let us be heard and you may do with us as you please. We only come here to hear mass, and so we beg you to sing it for us. When the mass is done and the sacrifice of praise, you may do as you please." The wolf, playing the part of a great priest, began to howl and shout aloud, so that the farmers, hearing the shouts and the howling of the wolf, came out well armed and with their dogs and gave him so many blows and wounds that he almost died, and he escaped well bitten by the dogs.

Fleeing thus, he reached a great stretch of road beneath a well branched tree, and throwing himself in the shade, worn out, he began to complain and curse, speaking to himself as follows: "Oh, Lord, how many evils have come upon me, and well deserved; for the most part they have been my fault. And where did my proud will lead me that I refused the lard and disdained the flesh of the pig? My father was no doctor, and I did not study medicine to cure a mare. My father was also no judge, neither did I learn law or legal principles, and who asked me to act the judge and judge between the sheep. Nor was my godfather a priest, nor did I learn my letters so that I should have to wash pigs in the sacred spring. Similarly it was a mad presumption that I should show myself as a priest and bishop to celebrate the divine offices." And reciting these misfortunes, he said a prayer, speaking thus: "O Jupiter, now let there fall from your ivory throne a knife that may strike me very hard." At this very moment there happened to be at the top of the tree a man trimming it, who listened carefully to all these words. And when the wolf ended his complaint and tale of troubles, the man threw the axe with which he was pruning the tree so that it struck the wolf in the nape of the neck and made him turn around. Getting up and looking at heaven and at the tree, he said: "O Jupiter, what great relics are contained here that so easily the prayers of those who pray and supplicate are heard? Now let this be known as the sacred place for all those who come here with their heart heavy, so that coming here they may be freed of tribulations." And dallying no longer, but running wounded and humiliated, the wolf returned to the woods from which he had come so proudly. This tale teaches us that a man should not wish to be called more than he is, nor should he desire greater things, nor be greater than his state permits. But each ought to be content with his place, and a man ought not to believe in auguries.

Fable 11. Of the Envious Dog

Some people are so envious they envy others for things they themselves cannot have and could not profit by. They stand in the way of others, as one may gather from this fable. A dog was lying in a manger full of hay. When the oxen came, he barked and snarled so fiercely they could not eat the hay. Then the ox said: "Look out, for you are doing wrong, perversely showing your envy of us. You can neither use nor profit by this hay, for dogs don't eat hay, yet you prevent us from eating our natural provender." Also the dog had a bone in his mouth that he could not chew, but he would not let any other dog enjoy it. This fable tells us that envy is hard to get rid of and those who are envious know not how to enjoy anything.

Fable 12. Of the Wolf and the Hungry Dog

If he who maintains a household and company does not feed his familiars well, he often suffers for his avarice. Similarly, he who exceeds his nature sometimes derives ill from it, as is shown in this fable.

A rich man had a huge flock of sheep and a dog who followed them to protect them from the wolves. But the man was stingy and did not feed the dog well. One day the wolf, coming up to the dog, remarked that he was very thin, and the reason must be that he was not well fed, for he knew the dog's master to be very stingy. Now if the dog wished, he would give him good advice in this matter. The dog answered: "I'll take whatever good advice you care to give me, for I am very thin." The wolf said: "What I think will do the trick for you is this: I will go in among the sheep and, taking one, will pretend to flee. You will follow me, and after you have run a long way you will pretend you are tired and will fall as if from weakness before you can catch me. The shepherds, seeing this, will then say: "If this dog of ours were better fed he would be stronger and the wolf could not steal one of our lambs. And I believe," said the wolf, "that you will get better and they will feed you adequately." The dog replied: "Do as you like."

Shortly the wolf took a sheep and began to run away with it. The dog followed after him, and before he could catch him he fell to the ground as if fainting from hunger. Seeing this, the shepherds and all the family said: "This dog has not had enough meat to eat, so he cannot run and catch the wolf. With his courage, if he were stronger and stouter, they couldn't steal a sheep and his hide. For this the master is to blame. Why does he not feed the dog as he should?" The master, hearing these things and showing that he was angry and ashamed, spoke thus: "May God curse those who have fed that dog, for I ordered him to be well fed, yet he is dying of hunger!" Thus he threw the blame on his family. But he said: "From now on give him meat in abundance." So after this gave him broth to eat from the kitchen and all the leavings of wheat, so that the dog began to take on some strength.

A few days later the wolf came again to the dog and said: "Brother, I gave you good advice." And the dog said: "It was indeed good advice, and needful for me." "Do you want some more good advice?" continued the wolf. "Yes," said the dog, "I will listen." "The advice is as follows," said the wolf: "Let us go among the sheep, and I will knock down one of the sheep and begin to run away with it. You will catch up with me and wound me in the chest in such a way that the wound is not serious, and then you will throw yourself on the ground like one who cannot stand up, being weak and thin in body, and then the shepherds will say: "If this dog were full and stuffed with good meat, the wolf would not get away with the sheep and wouldn't even escape with his life." The dog answered: "I am much afraid of my master who feeds me but does not fill me up, for I agree to what you say." Then entering the fold, the wolf took a fat sheep and began to run away with it down the road, and the dog followed him, as they had agreed, until he reached the wolf and wounded him in the chest fairly badly. Then he fell down like one who can do no more on account of hunger and weakness. The shepherds and all the company, seeing this, called out, saying: "Certainly if the dog were provided for to the point of contentment, the wolf would not carry off our fat sheep, nor would he escape alive." The master hearing this, with wrath and grief, said to them: "Look to it, for I order you to give the dog plenty to eat henceforth." And from then on they gave him cooked food with meat and good wheat bread, and so within a short time he took on his full strength, to the damage of his lord.

After a while the wolf came to the dog and said: "I gave you good advice this last time, brother." The dog replied: "I know it was good advice and useful and necessary for me." "I want to come in and take a sheep with your permission as a reward for what I have deserved," said the wolf. The dog replied: "You have had your thanks and wages, for you ate two of my lord and master's sheep." The wolf asked him again if he might take a sheep. Said the dog: "It does not please me, and if you do it, I swear by my life that you will not escape alive." When the wolf heard this he said: "Since that's the way you want it, give me some advice, for I am dying of hunger." To this the dog said: "Yesterday the wall of one of my master's rooms fell down, and there is to be found a great deal of bread and a lot of salt meat, and wine in abundance. If you go there tonight you can satisfy yourself with food." Said the wolf: "You are saying that to me deceitfully, for if I go in there you will give me away and warn your master and his company so they can kill me." "By my faith," said the dog, "I swear I will do no such thing; for my master's riches are not my responsibility except for the sheep. Therefore, I will not give you away." And with this assurance, as the night was dark, the wolf went to that room and filled himself with bread and fat meat. He even drank wine and got drunk and spoke thus, being pleased with himself: "These country folk, full of bread and wine, sing their songs, while I, though I cannot sing, am quite content." So he began to sing. The dogs, hearing his song, began to bark, but he continued his song, raising his voice. The men heard this and said: "The wolf is nearby." And when the wolf raised his voice even higher, they said: "For certain the wolf is singing in the pantry." So they all went there and found him singing. In no time at all the wolf was dead and finished off.

This fable teaches the rich and powerful that they should provide abundantly for their company, for if they fail to do so, even more will be stolen, so that the master will feel the loss each day. And it also shows us that a person should not exceed his own nature lest he incur danger as the wolf did here by drinking wine, which was not meant for his race, and became drunk and was killed because of it.

Fable 13. Of the Father and His Three Sons

Against those who bring suits and go before the judges for vain and negligible reasons this fable speaks.

At his death a man left three sons to whom he bequeathed all his possessions, that is, an apple tree, a goat, and a mill. After the father was buried the sons said: "Let us go before the judge and ask him to divide our inheritance." And they placed it before him in this manner: "Sir Judge, our father when he died left all three of us his possessions, share and share alike, to be divided by us." The judge asked what the possessions were, and they said: "A tree called an apple tree, a goat, and a mill." The judge said: "Well, how did he leave you the apple tree?" They replied: "He ordered it divided so that no one should have a larger part than any other." Said the judge: "How

are you going to divide the apple tree?" The oldest brother said: "I'll take all that is straight and crooked." The second said: "I will take what is green and dry." The third said: "I choose the roots with the trunk and branches." After hearing these words the judge said: "And who will get the most of it? Certainly neither I nor anyone else will be able to understand which of you will have the most or the least. And since this is so, whichever one of you who can declare that he has chosen the best part may have the whole tree."

Then the judge said: "And the goat? How did your father leave him to you?" They answered: "This is how he left the goat: That the one of us should inherit it who performed the greatest oratorical feat." Then the eldest brother spoke an oration as follows, saying: "Would God that this goat were so large that he might in one gulp drink up all the water in the sea with everything else under heaven and that even this might not be enough to satisfy him." The second brother said: "As I see it, the goat shall be mine, for by my prayer I will make the goat larger. So now let there be joined together every kind of wood, and every bush and tree and reed and flax, and all kinds of wool, and when a robe has been made of all this, let the goat be so large that the robe wouldn't be big enough to go around his leg." The third brother who spoke late and last said: "I believe the goat will be mine for I will make him large in this daring way. Oh, would to God there were a great eagle who would fly up to heaven and would look at all the four parts of the world, and as much breadth, length, and height as there is in this goat, so much might the eagle see." Having heard these petitions, the judge said: "I ask you which has made the most of the goat in his prayer, for I tell you that neither I nor anyone else would be able to determine it. Therefore let the goat belong to whichever one can truly declare this."

"But," said the judge: "What of the mill? How did your father ask to have it divided?" They answered: "Concerning the mill, he ordered in this fashion: he should have it who was held to be the greatest liar among the neighbors and relatives." And the eldest began to say that he ought to have it since he was the biggest liar among them, which he proved in this manner: "For many years I have been spending my time loafing in a large house, and through a single opening there fell upon my ear a drop of rain which has damaged the veins of my head, unnerving me and bringing pain to all my members, breaking my bones and rotting my brain, so that my brain marrow runs out my other ear, and because of this I am so weak I cannot get out of bed or turn over, nor bow my head by dint of great force in lying down." The second brother said: "As I see it, the mill should be mine as I am a far greater liar. For although I might fast for two weeks or even a month, if I came to a table laden with excellent victuals, I could not put a thing in my mouth because of my great habit of lying, unless others forced open my mouth and put food in it." The third said: "I really think the mill will be mine, for it is plain that I am the greatest liar. For even if I suffered from thirst to the point of death and was in water up to my neck, I would die without taking a single drop, if someone else opened my mouth by force and threw water into it." Then the judge said: "You do not know, and I do not understand, and there is no one in the world who can know, which of you is the biggest liar. Therefore I suspend the decision for now." So they went away without a judgment. This story teaches us that we should not take up suits or go into court for vain and trivial things or matters that are so obscure and difficult they cannot be determined by judgment. And let us not be mocked and spend our resources uselessly as these three brothers did.

Fable 14. Of the Vixen and the Wolf

Those who prefer to be teachers rather than pupils and try first to teach rather than be taught, wishing to become equal to those greater and more learned than themselves, fall into great errors and evil: that is what this story teaches and demonstrates.

The vixen, going with her son to the wolf, begged him in this manner: "My Lord Wolf, I graciously ask to wash my son in this sacred fountain, and I ask you to be his godfather." The wolf replied: "I will gladly do that." And he did so. And after the little fox was washed, they gave him the name Benitillo. In a little while the wolf said to the vixen, his gossip: "I beg you, sister, to leave your son Benitillo, my godson, to grow up with me. He will be

taught and indoctrinated in all the arts I know. And he will grow up better with me because you have many children, and you rear them all with great difficulty." The vixen replied: "My lord, do as you see fit, and I thank you very much for thinking of me." Leaving little Benitillo with the wolf, the mother returned to her other children.

One day, taking his apprentice Benitillo with him, the wolf passed by some corrals where there was a flock of sheep, intending to seize one of them. But because he was discovered by the dogs and the shepherds, he could not capture any of them. So at dawn he went up to a high mountain above a town and said to his protégé, Benitillo: "You know that this evening I went for the sheep, and now I am tired and worn out. You keep watch while I sleep and watch when the animals come out of the town on their way to pasture. You must wake me when you see them come out, for we will get something to eat." The wolf slept until morning, when his godson woke him, calling: "Sir, Sir," and the godfather said to him, "What do you want, godson?" And he answered: "The swine are coming out." And the wolf said: "We do not care about them, for they are dirty and nasty creatures. When I eat them they give me cramps, and even worse, their bristles or hairs often clog my throat and get stuck there." Later, about six in the morning, Benitillo called: "Sir godfather." The wolf replied: "What is it, godson?" He replied: "See the cows coming out to pasture." The wolf said: "I don't care about them, for the cowherds who guard them are strong and cruel and bring along fierce and evil mastiffs. When they smell me, they bark, and they pursue me to the death."

At nine o'clock Benitillo called the wolf: "Sir, already the mares are coming out." The wolf ordered him to watch where they were going, and the little fox watched them and returned to report that they were going into a meadow near the poplar forest. Hearing this, the wolf arose and set out carefully and prudently. He entered the woods by such a route that no one saw him, and he arrived secretly at the meadow where the mares were grazing. Then he leaped up and took the fattest one by the nostrils and killed her by choking, and thus he feasted on her, he and his apprentice Benitillo. And when the little fox felt full, he came up to the wolf, saluted him, and said, "Sir, godfather, if there is anything you want done I will do it gladly, and I will obey your command. Because I feel sufficient and know what I need to know to earn my living, I beg permission to go and see my mother, for I do not need to know more and am satisfied." The wolf answered: "Son, I do not want you to go, for I know that you will be sorry if you go too soon and will repent of it." The godson replied: "Since I know what I want, I shall remain here no longer." As the wolf saw that he was determined to go, he said to him: "Go in peace. But I must tell you that before long you will be sorry. But since you wish it you must greet my gossip, your mother, for me."

The little fox went to his mother, who, when she saw him, said: "Why have you left your school so soon?" Little Benitillo answered: "I come because I am well and adequately taught. I have learned so much that I can support not only you and me but all your children without difficulty." His mother asked him: "Son, where did you learn so quickly?" He answered her: "You do not need to bother about knowing and learning that, but get up and follow me and you will see that I am a good teacher." The mother, although she had no confidence, still, to please him, followed her son. Benitillo, as he had seen the wolf do, went by night to the sheep to capture one of them, but as he could not, he went to a high mountain near a town and said to his mother: "You remember how tonight I went to the sheep pens. I am now tired and worn out and I shall sleep a little, and you watch out and look when the animals come out to graze. When you see them, wake me up, and then you will see what I know and what I have learned, for I want to show you my skills and learning." Near morning the vixen began to call her son: "Benitillo." He answered: "What do you want, mother?" She said: "Note that the swine are coming out to pasture." The son answered: "Let's not pay any attention to them, for they are dirty and tiresome and full of bristles and they cause indigestion to those who eat them, and they clog the palate." At the hour of six, the mother called her son, Benitillo, who said: "Why don't you let me sleep a bit, for you know I am tired?" She said to him: "The cows are coming out of the town." He said: "I do not care for them, for they are well guarded, and the cowherds are strong and the dogs are ferocious, and when they see me, they bark and chase me until I can stand it no more." Afterwards, at nine o'clock, the mother called the son telling him to get up. The little fox said: "What is going on?" His mother said: "The mares are coming out to pasture." To this Benitillo replied joyfully: "Look, mother, and see where they are going." The mother looked again, and said: "They have gone into some meadows near the woods." Then Benitillo arose and said to his mother: "You stay here on top of the mountain and watch what I do, and you will see truly my knowledge and skill." So he went into the woods slyly so that he was not seen by anyone, and he reached the place where the mares were grazing. He jumped on one of the fattest and took her by the nostrils, thinking to choke and kill her easily and do to her as his master the wolf had. But the mare hardly felt his weight. Lifting young Benitillo, she began to run toward the cowherds with the young fox hanging from her nose, where his teeth were clamped. And the mother, seeing this from the mountain, began to call, "O son, Benitillo, let go the mare and come this way in safety." But he, being unable to let go the animal because his teeth were fastened into its nostrils, was carried away by force. And when the vixen saw the cowherds come running, knowing they were going to kill her son, she struck one paw against the other and began to call out and weep, saying: "Woe to you, my son Benitillo! Why did you come back from your studies so soon? I see that they are now going to kill you. Thus you will leave your mother woebegone and in grief. You should have listened to the words of the wolf, your good godfather." Thus young Benitillo was caught and killed by the cowherds. This story teaches us that no one should presume to be master until he has been a student, and he should not teach before learning, nor ought he pretend to be equal to others greater and more learned than he.

Fable 15. Of the Wolf, the Dog, and the Sheep

Sometimes simple deceivers with little ability, studying and striving to deceive the wise and powerful, deceive and hurt themselves, as this story shows.

There was once a man who had great flocks of sheep and other livestock. And he had on guard a huge, formidable mastiff to frighten the wolves, making them flee out of fear of him. On account of this ferocious dog no wolf dared draw near the sheep. But after many years it came to pass that he died, and the shepherds, upset by this, said: "What shall we do now that we have lost that great mastiff? He made our field safe. From now on the wolves will come and destroy our sheep." Hearing this, a conceited sheep said to the shepherds: "Listen to a wise counsel: cut off my horns and clip my wool, and dress me in the very hide of the dead dog, and I will frighten all the wolves by the sight of me, for they will think that I am the dog." The shepherds took his advice and dressed the sheep in the hide of the dog. Then the wolves, when they saw the sheep dressed in the skin of the dog, all fled in great fear. But one day a wolf arrived there very hungry, and seizing a lamb he began to escape with it. The sheep in the dog's skin, seeing this, ran after the wolf, who believed it was the dog and beshat himself for fear. So he began to run with greater speed, at which the sheep followed him more determinedly. The wolf, in great anxiety beshat himself again because of his fear of the sheep in dog's guise. Finally the wolf, realizing that he could flee no more nor escape, doubled over with fear, and so he beshat himself a third time very foully, sowing evil seed along the road. And so in great anxiety to save his life, the wolf ran with the sheep following close behind. And while both of them were running in this fashion it happened that thorns near the road tore the dog skin in which the sheep was dressed, and then there appeared from beneath the skin and wool of the sheep. The wolf then understood the deception, and turning back captured the sheep and asked him: "Who are you?" And the sheep, unable to deny it, said: "I am a sheep." To which the wolf said: "And why did you frighten me so?" And the sheep answered: "I did it as a joke and was playing with you." To this the wolf said: "Follow me and I will teach you a game." And taking him to the first place where he had beshat himself for fear, he showed it to him and said: "Does this seem to you a good game?" Then he took him to the second and the third places where he had beshat himself for fear, and asked him again: "Does this seem to you a good game, that a wolf for fear and terror of a sheep should have had to dirty and beshit himself three times?" For punishment for his game, the wolf then beheaded the sheep and ate him.

This fable means that the unimportant and ignorant should not presume to deceive the learned and powerful lest finally they deceive themselves.

Fable 16. Of the Little Man, the Lion, and His Cub

Those who will not heed their fathers and mothers nor accept their principles and teachings get into many troubles and dangers, as this parable teaches.

A little man dwelt in a deserted place, living by his work and the efforts of his hands, cutting down trees and sowing the land and the fields. And a lion who wandered about in that wilderness destroyed his grain and cereals and tore up his plants and orchards and did him many other sorts of harm. The little man, seeing all this damage that the lion caused him, thought of as many evil tricks against him as he could. And he set up nets and snares in as many ways as he could think of. The lion, knowing that he could not escape so many tricks and snares, took his small cub and went to another region where he could live in greater safety than where he had lived, where he suffered fear and worry.

After a long time the lion cub, now grown big and strong, asked his father one day if they were native to the region where they now dwelt or whether they had come from elsewhere and were strangers. The father answered: "We are not of this kingdom. We are of another province, and we came to this land fleeing from the snares and nets of a little man." The lion's son asked: "Who is this little man who frightens lions?" The father answered: "He is not so big or strong as we are, but he is very clever and ingenious." The little lion said: "Since that is the case, I will go there and avenge our injuries." The father begged him in no fashion to go there, for he knew the many tricks of the man and that his son would not be able to catch him by any trick or snare to kill him. The son answered, saying this: "By my head and soul, I shall do no less than I say, and I shall avenge our injuries." Said the father, "Son, do not go there. If you do not believe me, you will be sorry for it." But the little lion paid no attention to what his father advised. He went to seek out the little man.

Going along the road, he encountered a horse grazing in a field. His back was stripped of hair and his ribs had been broken, he asked the horse: "Tell me who hurt you so cruelly." The horse answered: "The little man ties me with various knots and fastenings of iron and wood and bridles me, and he rides me and makes me run wherever he wills, and thus he wears the hair off my back, and he breaks my ribs by making me work until I am almost dead." Said the lion: "You are my father's horse." The horse answered: "And also yours through your father." At this the lion spoke very ferociously as follows: "By my head, I will avenge your injuries."

Going a little farther he met an ox, badly wounded and bearing marks of the goad, grazing in a meadow, of whom he asked: "By whom were you so severely injured, friend?" The ox replied: "The little man ties me up with strong straps and makes me plow the land and drag stones, wounding me almost to the death." Said the lion: "And you are my father's ox." The ox said: "Not only your father's but yours also, sir." For this the little lion grumbled to himself, saying, "Oh, how many evils has this little man committed, not only against me but against mine! By my beard I will avenge myself on him." Looking at the ground, he saw the tracks of the little man, and he asked the ox: "Whose tracks are these?" To which the ox replied: "These are the tracks of the little man." Then the lion, extending his pad upon the track, said: "How small a foot the little man has, and yet he does so many evils!" And so he asked the ox to point out the little man to him. The ox said: "There he is," and pointed with his hoof.

The lion looked and saw the man, who was on a hill holding in his hand a spade with which he was digging the earth. Approaching him the lion said: "O little man, how many evils have you committed against me and against my father and against our beasts whose kings we are? Now it is right that you should make amends and that I avenge myself upon you." The little man, showing him a rod, an axe, and a knife, said: "Thus do I swear to God who made me and upon the soul of my father that if you come up here I will kill you with my rod, and that with this axe I will cut you up, and with this knife I will make pieces of your hide." The lion replied in great fear, since the man had such great daring: "Since you don't want me to climb to where you are nor to serve justice on you, let us go, you and I, to my father and let him judge between us which should be king." The little man replied: "Swear solemnly that you will commit no harm against me while we are on the way, and I shall swear the same. And so it will please me to go." With this the little lion swore not to undertake anything against him during this time, and the little man swore not to touch him. This pact and agreement concluded, they set out on their way. But the little man left the high road and took the path in which he had his snares prepared. And the lion said to him: "I want to follow along the road you travel." The man replied: "As you will." And going thus with the lion behind him, the latter fell suddenly into a snare in which he was caught and fastened by two feet. Then with a loud voice he called to the little man to help him. The man asked what was wrong and the lion replied: "I don't know what has caught me by the feet so I beg you to help me." And the little man said: "You know that I swore not to touch you anywhere on this road until we heard the sentence of your father, so I cannot help you." Then, as the lion went on with his feet tied, in a little while he fell into another snare, in which his forepaws were tightly tied so that he could not move, and so he began to call to the little man asking him to help. But the man, instead of helping him, took a green stick from the woods and began to beat him cruelly. The lion said to the little man: "Have pity on me and pardon me. Do not strike me on the head or in the back or the stomach, but strike me on the ears that did not listen to my father's advice, and in the heart. I refused to listen to his good teaching in which he told me that you had many tricks of which I would repent." So the little man struck the lion in the ears and in the heart until he killed him. This fable teaches us to be obedient to our parents and to keep their commandments and teachings and to heed their advice.

Fable 17. Of the Knight, the Vixen, and the Squire

This fable teaches us that there are many persons who extend themselves so far in lying that, knowing their hearers do not believe them, they contradict little by little what they have said.

A knight, riding with his squire, saw a vixen and said: "O Lord, what a large vixen I see." And looking at it his squire said: "You marvel, Sir, at this vixen? By the faith I owe you, I have been in a region where I saw a vixen bigger than an ox." The knight said: "Oh how one could trim priests' cassocks or the habits of nuns with such skins, so large they are." So they went their way and relaxed their reins in order to tell many fables. The knight said: "O Jupiter all powerful, I beg you to keep us this day from all lies and help us to pass over this dangerous river without harm to our bodies and take us safely to the place and the inn we want to reach." The squire, hearing these words, asked the knight: "Sir, I beg you to tell me what moves you to beg and to pray so devoutly." Replied the knight: "How is it that you do not know what is obvious? Now we have to pass over a river that is of great virtue and marvel, and if anyone who goes into it has that day lied he cannot come out alive, but rather he will be drowned in it." Hearing this, the squire was much afraid and disturbed. When they reached a ditch, the squire asked: "Sir, is this the dangerous river of which you were speaking?" "No," he replied, "this is not it. We are not yet near it." And the squire said: "For this reason I maintain that the vixen of which I spoke today was no larger than an ass." The lord answered: "I do not care how big the vixen was." And, going on their way, they came to another river. And the squire asked: "Sir, this must be the river of which you were speaking." The knight answered: "We have not yet reached it." The squire spoke, saying: "I ask you because I remember that I spoke of a vixen as big as a donkey, but now I wish to change my statement, for she was no bigger than a calf." The lord replied: "I have no interest in the fox, whether it be large or small." Finally they came to another river. The squire from the worry that beset him began to speak: "This must be the river of danger." The knight replied: "We have not yet reached it." The squire spoke again: "Because of all I said about that vixen today I now say this: certainly it was no bigger than a lamb." The lord, considering all the squire had spoken, said to him: "Don't bother me with your vixen, but talk about something else."

In the afternoon when they reached a great river, the squire said: "Now I think this must be the river of which we spoke." And the lord said: "That is true, for this is the river of great marvels." The squire spoke in great fear and much ashamed as follows: "Sir, I confess to you that I lied about that vixen, for I swear on my head that the vixen I saw in that other region was no bigger than the one we saw today." Then the knight, jokingly and laughing and scolding him, said to him: "And I also swear to you that the water of this river is no worse and no more dangerous than any other water."

This fable admonishes and warns liars not to lie too much, and to reform themselves, for many times they give themselves away and are betrayed by the prudent to whom they contradict themselves, revoking their lies by their own mouths.

Here end the remarkable ancient fables of Aesop.
I do not know whether they are attributed to him properly or wrongly.

VI. The Fables of Aesop
from the Translation of Remitius

Here follow some fables of Aesop from the new translation by Remitius.

Fable 1. Of the Eagle and the Crow

The eagle, flying from a lofty crag, swooped down and took a lamb from a flock of sheep, carrying it on high. The crow, seeing this and moved by envy, flew against a lamb with a great racket and crying out, thinking to take and lift the lamb as the eagle had done. And he turned around and struck his claws into the lamb's wool, so that however much he beat his wings he could not work himself free from the fleece. When the shepherd saw him thus caught in the wool, he ran and caught the crow, and cutting his wings he gave the crow to his children to play with. When one of them asked him what sort of bird it was, he replied, "In my heart I was an eagle, but as I now know, I am a crow." This fable tells us that he who dares to go beyond his own strength often falls upon ill fortune and becomes a laughingstock.

Fable 2. Of the Eagle and the Beetle

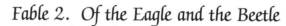

The eagle followed a rabbit to catch it, and she could not escape because she saw no one to appeal to for her defense. Finally she saw a beetle and asked it for help, telling him she had no other defenders. The beetle took her under his protection, promising he would defend her. At this moment he saw the eagle approaching and appealed to him very affectionately not to bother or kill the rabbit, who had commended herself to his protection. The eagle, scorning the small size of the beetle, paid him no heed, but in his presence seized and killed the rabbit. The beetle, feeling himself insulted, followed him and managed to find where the eagle had his nest. In time the eagle laid her eggs, and when the beetle learned this he climbed up and flew to the eagle's nest, where he cast her eggs to the ground. The eagle, moved by her grief and regret at losing her eggs, flew to Jupiter, for she was a bird very sacred to that god, and she asked him to send her to a safe and sure place to lay her eggs. Jupiter authorized her, when the proper time came, to lay them in his very own bosom. The beetle, when he heard this, watched to see when the eagle laid her eggs, and when she laid them he flew up with a pellet of manure and let the pellet fall in the very bosom of Jupiter, where the eggs lay. Wishing to cast away the manure on his breast, Jupiter threw down the eggs with it. And from then on it is said that the eagle does not lay her eggs where there are beetles. This fable means it is not wise to injure anyone, no matter how small he may be, for there is no one injured who will not take vengeance in due time.

Fable 3. Of the Vixen and the Goat

Men of good sense look at the end result before they begin an affair they intend to carry out, as we gather from this fable. The vixen and the goat, wishing to get a drink, went down to a fountain or well. And after they had satisfied their thirst they looked for a way to get out of the well, which was difficult. Considering this, the vixen said: "Brother, listen to my advice, for I have thought of a way to get out of here in safety. If you will stand on your feet and approach the wall with your horns, I will climb on your back and horns and thus get out, and when I am on top I will take you by the hand and with my help you will get out." The goat, taking the vixen's advice, did as he had been persuaded. But the vixen, once safely out of the well, made fun of the goat. The goat then reminded the vixen of the contract between them that she did not wish to fulfill, insisting that she carry out her agreement. She replied: "O courteous goat: If you had been as provided with wisdom and prudence as you are with an abundance of beard, you would not have gone down in to the well without looking out for a way to exit." And so this fable signifies that the prudent and sensible man should think of the end before beginning the task.

Fable 4. Of the Cat and the Rooster

This fable treats of men of evil nature and condition. The cat had caught a rooster and was looking for a chance to kill and eat him. And he began to accuse the rooster, saying that he was a bird who annoyed and disturbed everyone, not letting them sleep at night. The rooster excused himself, saying that he did that for the profit of all, for he awoke them so they might get up to do their duty. The cat said more to the rooster: "You are cruel and mean and atrociously wicked, for you act against nature by having relations with your mother and sisters, recognizing no debt or relationship whatever." To this the rooster replied that he did it to give profit to his master, for without that coitus and intervention of his the hens laid no eggs. Then the cat said: "Although you have many excuses, in spite of them I do not intend to fast." This fable says that one who is evil and perverse by nature, when he decides in his heart to do evil, even though no valid reason moves him, does not fail to carry out his intention.

Fable 5. Of the Vixen and the Bramble Bush

It is madness to ask help from those who by their nature come to impede and not to help, of which this fable is a brief example. A vixen climbed a fence to escape from the danger she found herself in, for dogs were following her, and she embraced a bramble whereby her paws were lacerated. When she saw herself gravely hurt by the thorns of the blackberry she said: "I seized you so that you might help me, and you do me more harm than the enemy." To this the bramble replied: "Friend, you were wrong, for you thought to take me by deception, as you are accustomed to take other things." This says that it is a foolish person who asks help from one who is most inclined by nature to do evil and harm rather than to help.

Fable 6. Of the Man and the Wooden God

This fable proves that one should not do evil, even if sometimes it is profitable, except under force of necessity. A man who had a wooden god in his house begged and prayed to it to do him some good. But the more he begged and prayed, the less good and profit he had in his house, and his distress and poverty increased every day. Finally, in great anger, he took his wooden god by the legs and banged its head against the wall, thus breaking it. A lot of gold fell out, and the man, picking up the gold, said to his god: "Very perverse and cruel you are, and stubborn, for you refused to do me any good while I held you in honor and reverence. Now that I have struck and

dishonored you greatly, you have been good to me." This signifies that the evil man does no good and is useful only by force.

Fable 7.　Of a Fisherman

All things are done well that are done at their proper time, as this fable demonstrates. A fisherman who was not expert in the art of fishing came to the edge of the sea with flutes, trumpets, and nets. And seating himself upon a stone or crag, he first began to play the trumpet and flutes as loudly as he could, thinking that in this way he would catch fish more easily. But discovering that the sound of the trumpet and flutes brought no success, he put them down and cast his net into the sea and caught a lot of fish. When he took them out of the net and saw how they jumped, the fisherman said courteously: "O ignorant creatures! When I played the flute and trumpet you did not wish to dance. Now that I do not play, why do you want to dance and jump?" And thus are all things done at the proper time.

Fable 8. Of the Mice and the Cat

This fable proves that the sensible and prudent man, if once deceived by someone, forever after disbelieves deceitful and false men. A cat, realizing that in a certain house there were many mice, went after them and caught and ate a lot of them, one after another. But the mice, realizing that day after day they were being consumed and their number lessened, joined together and said it was not safe for them henceforth downstairs. They agreed to dwell upstairs where the cat could not climb so that they might not all be caught. The cat, understanding the agreement of the mice, pretended that he was dead and he hanged himself by the feet from a long pole which was close to a wall. One of the mice up above, looking at him sharply, said: "Ay, friend, even if I knew you were caught in a bellows, or wind-maker, never would I come down from here." This fable means that he who has been fooled once should not believe false pretenders.

Fable 9. Of the Farmer and the Bustard

He who is found in the company of the evil receives a punishment equal to theirs, as this fable teaches. A farmer placed snares in his field to catch cranes and geese because they destroyed his wheat and seedlings. And with them he caught a bustard which, seeing himself trapped, asked the farmer to let him go and send him away, for he was not of the family of geese or cranes but a bustard, which is one of the most pious among all the birds because he never fails to protect his mother and father in their old age, but at all times serves them. The farmer, smiling, said to him: "What you say does not escape me nor am I ignorant, and I hold that you are good, but you were caught in the company of these cranes and geese which have damaged my field, and it is right that you should die with them for you are as guilty as they are." This fable says that we should avoid all evil company.

Fable 10. Of the Boy Who Tended the Sheep

He who is infamous as a liar, although he tells the truth, is not believed, concerning which look at this fable. A shepherd, pasturing his sheep in a

high and lofty place, often called for help in order to play a joke on those who worked and plowed in neighboring fields, shouting "Wolf!" Those who were in the neighborhood, hearing the shouts, left their work and came to his aid. But finding no wolf they returned to their work. The shepherd excused himself, saying that the wolves had fled to parts unknown. When the lad had played this game several times, one day the wolf really did come and went among the sheep. So the boy began to yell for help, as before: "Wolf! Wolf!" But the farmers, thinking he was joking, as on other occasions, made no effort to help him. So the wolf destroyed and killed as many sheep as he wished. This happened to the lying shepherd because on other occasions he had lied, and so they did not believe him when he truly needed help.

Fable 11. Of the Ant and the Dove

This fable means that because dumb animals show their gratitude toward those who are kind to them, how much more ought men who have reason express their thanks toward those from whom they receive favors. A very thirsty ant went to drink at a spring, where by chance he fell into the water. It happened that at this moment there was a dove up in a tree. Seeing that the ant was drowning, the dove very quickly broke off a little branch with his beak and threw it into the water, and the ant got on the branch and escaped from the water. While the two of them were still there, a dove hunter came by and began to ready his nets and snares and decoys to capture that dove. The ant, seeing this, bit the hunter's foot, and the hunter, feeling the

pain in his foot, left his contraptions and went away. The dove, seeing him depart, flew away from the tree and thus escaped. This tale means that no one should be ungrateful toward him from whom he has received a benefit.

Fable 12. Of the Bee and Jupiter

It sometimes happens, as this fable shows, that when we pray for some evil to befall our enemies, the same evil happens to ourselves. The bee, which is the mother of wax, one time went to sacrifice to the gods and offered honey to Jupiter. He, very happy with her sacrifice, ordered that she should be given whatever favor she asked. The bee, knowing that Jupiter was very kindly disposed toward her, begged in this manner: "O most illustrious and excellent and distinguished god of the gods, I beg before your excellent majesty that you grant your servant this grace and favor: that whenever anyone comes to the hive to steal or take honey by force, I may sting him so that he will die forthwith." Jupiter, who loved the race of man, carefully considered this request and finally ordered as follows: "It is enough that you shall sting whoever steals honey from the hive, and in the sting you will leave the stinger, and then you yourself will die, so that your stinger will mean your life to you." Thus he turned upon the bee the evil she demanded for others. This fable signifies that one should not seek evil for others, for the evil that comes from his mouth will end up in his own bosom.

Fable 13. Of a Woodcutter

The kinder God is to the good, the crueler he is to the evil, as you will see in the following story. On the bank of a river dedicated to the god Mercury, a woodchopper dropped the axe with which he was cutting wood into the river. The poor woodchopper, seeing himself without the axe with which he earned his living, began to weep and groan in great anguish on the bank of the river,

asking Mercury to help him in his need. Hearing this, Mercury, moved by
pity, appeared to the woodchopper and asked the reason for his great sorrow
and weeping. Having heard the cause, Mercury brought the woodcutter an
axe of gold and asked him if this was the axe he had lost. He replied that
certainly this was not the axe that had fallen into the river. Then Mercury
showed him another axe that was made of silver, which the woodchopper
also denied was his. The third time Mercury offered the woodchopper his
own axe made of iron, and the woodchopper, recognizing it, affirmed that
this was his axe. Mercury, seeing that the poor man was just and truthful,
gave him all three axes together. Taking the three axes, the gold, the silver,
and his own, the woodchopper went to his companions and told them of his
good fortune.

One of his companions, moved by greed and desiring some good fortune,
went to that river, threw in an axe that he had, and sat down weeping and
complaining on the bank, making loud cries. The god Mercury appeared to
him, asking the reason for his sorrow. He wept and declared the cause of his
adversity, and accordingly Mercury first brought him a gold axe, asking if
that was the axe he had lost. Because of his greed, he said without hesitation
that it was his axe. Mercury, seeing his impudence, his shameless lie, and
his uncontrolled eagerness, gave the man neither the gold axe nor his own
which he had thrown into the river. And so the gods reward goodness and
punish evil.

Fable 14. Of the Thieving Boy and His Mother

He who is not punished at the start, when he first commences to go astray and do evil, gets worse day after day, as this fable proves. Half in jest, a boy who was learning his letters stole a book that a companion was reading and took it to his mother who, instead of punishing and reproving him for his crime, received the book with pleasure. A little while later he stole from another companion a cloak, which he also took to his mother, who received it with pleasure. Each day the unpunished boy stole something and assumed thieving as a trade. Because the boy had stolen many things and some important ones, one day he was caught in an obvious theft and was captured and tortured. His past revealed, the boy was sentenced and condemned to be hanged like the thief that he was. And as the townspeople were taking him to the place of punishment, his mother came weeping and complaining. He asked permission to speak a word to her secretly, and turning towards her ear, as if to speak secretly, he bit it off with his teeth. The mother, complaining of the pain, cursed and spoke against her son. Then those who were leading him, taking his action for great disobedience lawlessness, accused him not only of the theft but of the cruelty he had committed against his mother. The shameless thief said: "Do not marvel that I have bitten off my mother's ear, because she was the cause of the evil I now suffer and of all my misfortunes. For if she had punished me when I brought home the stolen book, I would have ceased to steal, and I would not come to be hanged as a thief." This fable shows that children are to be punished and reprehended when they commit a crime or misdeed so that they may not proceed to great crimes.

Fable 15. Of the Flea

This fable teaches that the evils that predominate and never cease deserve no pity, even when their error or sin is small. A flea was caught while biting a man. Being thus caught, she was asked by the man: "What are you that bite me thus in the legs?" She answered: "I am of the lineage of animals whose nature it is to bite people and to live in this way. Therefore I beg you to pardon me and not to kill me, for you know that the evil I commit is small and that I cannot do much harm." The man, smiling, replied: "For that reason you will die at my hands, for your nature is not inclined to good works, nor is it suitable for you to annoy people, whether much or little." And thus it is shown that we are not to pardon those who do evil even though their crime is small. Because they are accustomed to do evil, one must all the more consider the will as a deed and crime committed.

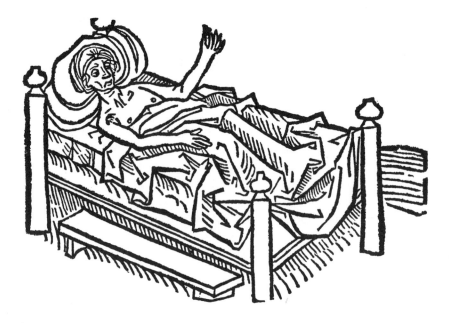

Fable 16. Of the Husband and the Two Wives

There is nothing better for the health of the old than not to have wives, especially young wives, as this fable shows. It was summertime, when the generative principle is most active, and a middle aged and nearly gray-haired man, accustomed to pleasures and joys took two wives—one old and one young, dwelling together in one house. To attract her husband to her love, the old one deloused his head every day and pulled out his black hairs so that he might seem older and would more closely resemble her aged appearance. The younger woman, in order to take him away from the company of the other wife and win his love, began to pull out her husband's gray hairs, thinking to turn him thus more toward youth. Finally he was made so bald by the two of them that he became the laughingstock and object of mirth of the whole town. And so it seems that it is very healthy for old men not to have wives unless they want to live in constant affliction and torment and be buried alive. Therefore keep yourself celibate, for you will become not partly grayhaired but totally so.

Fable 17. Of the Farmer and His Sons

Constant labor brings treasure, as this fable demonstrates. A farmer, knowing that he had come to the end of his days and desiring that his sons should be instructed in the work of their land, called them to him and said: "Sons, I leave all my worldly goods in our vineyard; so whenever you desire to share among yourselves, look for the goods in it and there you will find them." Not long after the father died the sons went to the vineyard to look for his worldly goods, saying that they must find some treasure in the vineyard. And so they dug up the vineyard deeply with spades and suitable tools, but they found there no treasure at all, as they had thought they would. But as the vineyard was very well spaded, it gave forth more fruit that year than it had previously in two years combined, and thus the sons profited much by it and became rich. This means that every day's work is in itself a treasure.

Here end the fables of Aesop taken from Remitius, composer of the new translation of the Greek fables, which are not contained in the four books dictated by Romulus.

VII. The Fables of Avianus

Here begin the fables of Avianus.

Fable 1. Of the Village Woman and the Wolf

Those who heed women's words are oftimes deceived, as you will hear in the following fable. The wolf, pained by hunger, once left his woods seeking food for himself, his wife, and his young. He approached a house as quietly as he could in the hope of getting some meat when he heard the voice of a mother saying to her bitterly weeping son: "If you do not quiet down I will throw you to the mad wolf for him to eat you." The wolf, believing these words, waited all night in the hope that the woman would give him her son as she had promised, but the boy, after crying a great deal, grew tired and fell asleep. Because of this, the wolf lost all hope, and his hunger made him turn back to the woods to his wife and youngsters. When the she-wolf realized he was returning hungry and worn out, she said to him: "How did it happen that you bring no game or prey, as you usually do, but instead come here sad and with your mouth open?" To this the wolf replied: "Do not wonder that I bring no prey or game, for I was detained by a woman all night, hoping for food on the basis of her words, and thus did daylight catch up with me. And as I was seen by all the villagers and their dogs, I barely escaped. When I went seeking some meat for us, I was promised a small boy, but he was not given to me. In this hope I waited in danger until now." From this, one may conclude that if one does not wish to be deceived, he ought not to give credence and faith to the inconstancy of women.

Fable 2. Of the Tortoise or Turtle and the Birds

One cannot climb to lofty heights without great effort, and the higher one climbs by his own power the farther down he can fall, as this fable testifies. When all the birds were gathered together a tortoise came among them, saying: "If one of you will raise me up, I will certainly show him the shells in which many precious stones grow, which I cannot reach by myself even if I were to move unceasingly, for I walk very little and with my slow pace I do not go very far." The birds were delighted by the tortoise's offer even though it was deceitful. They appointed the eagle, the bird which flies highest and fastest, to take the tortoise up. The eagle, taking the tortoise in her talons, flew up high in the air where she asked the tortoise to show her, as promised, the shells that grew the precious stones. As the tortoise could not do this, the eagle began to squeeze her with her sharp talons. And the tortoise, groaning, said: "I would not have suffered these torments if I had not asked to be raised up in the air." On hearing these words, the eagle let go of her, and the tortoise, whom nature had so strongly armed, fell to earth and was broken to pieces. This fable warns that each of us should be content with the status that nature gave him, for pride rarely results in a good end but rather leads to a fall.

Fable 3. Of the Two Lobsters or Crayfish

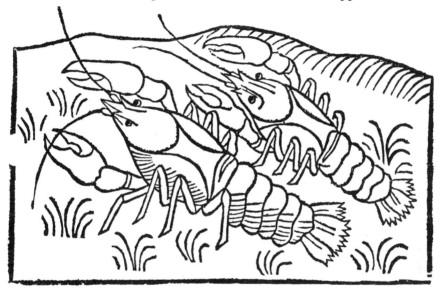

No one should accuse another of a sin or vice that he has not first corrected in himself, as this fable notes. A lobster or crayfish noticed that her daughter was walking crookedly and did not carry her feet straight. In doing so, the daughter ground herself against the sharp stones in the water. So that her daughter might go straight and without harm, the mother said: "Beloved daughter, do not walk about on these rough paths which are not plainly marked, and watch that you do not walk so crookedly, but walk straight and handsomely and you will not hurt yourself so much." The daughter answered: "Mother, you first walk forward nicely so that I may see how you move, and I will follow in your steps as best I can." The mother began to walk, and the daughter saw that her mother went crookedly and clumsily, as she herself did. She said to her mother: "I wonder how you can say I walk clumsily when you yourself do not know how to walk any better." And so this tale demonstrates how silly and ill-seeming it is for one person to reproach another for the same faults he possesses.

Fable 4. Of the Ass in the Lion's Skin

Every man should help himself by his own means and not depend on others. By doing so, he may not be deceived and teased when he loses the belongings of others, which he had presumptuously and improperly usurped, as this fable shows us clearly. An ass, finding a lion skin, put it on and covered his members as best he could. In the dress of the honored lion, which was far more decorated than the ass's had ever been, the ass frightened the other animals. With a new-found presumption, the ass sniffed and trampled on the food of the sheep and lambs and frightened the peaceful animals like the deer and rabbit in the woods. While he was strutting in this fashion, the villager who had lost him chanced to pass through the same woods. He found the ass dressed in the skin and took him by the long ears, which the ass could not cover, and beat him cruelly with sticks, stripping him of the lion's skin, and saying to him lightly: "You frighten others easily and intimidate those who do not know you, but you cannot frighten those who know you, for as you were, are, and will remain a jackass dressed in the garments of your father. Do not covet the honor of others which does not belong to you so that you may not be ridiculed when they take away that with which you sought improperly to honor yourself."

Fable 5. Of the Frog Who Was a Doctor and the Vixen

One should never praise himself for knowing things that in fact he does not know and cannot profit from unless he wishes to incur harm. That is what

this fable means. The frog, born and raised in the depths of the waters and dwelling in the lagoons all his life, went out into the green and flowering meadow where the animals were, saying that she was a great physician and skilled in the art of medicine. She offered to cure all ills and even to preserve life better than Peonius, the greatest of doctors, who was said to have made the gods immortal. But the simple beasts, believing the frog's mad words, gave credence to her boasting and vain eloquence. When the vixen, who was cleverer than the rest of the animals, heard what the frog had promised, she said to them: "Oh what great folly is this? I marvel that you foolishly believe that this frog can cure any disease, however slight it may be, since she herself is yellow and hydropic. If she were the doctor she says she is, she would have first cured herself and cast away the wrinkles with which she is covered so that she might be believed. Since her ugliness is far from the knowledge for which she wishes to be praised and her works are very unlike her words, let us pay no attention to her soft speech, for self-praise does not ring true in her mouth." The frog, ashamed and hearing her learning mocked, left the meadow. This story teaches that one should not quickly believe those who praise themselves and say they know many things. Rather, one should guard against them as against the alchemists who commonly go about hungry and in tatters without faculties and claim to enrich others while they do not know how to earn enough to feed themselves. They do nothing to avoid idleness but throw coals in the fire, saying that they will perform marvelous deeds.

Fable 6. Of the Two Dogs

It is difficult to recognize those who are of a perverse heart. If anything happens to them, it is reputed to them as an honor or dishonor, as this fable declares. There was once a man who had a dog who did not bark or growl, but with his tail between his legs, he treacherously bit people. Knowing the dog's habits, his master, so that no one might be unaware of the dog's deception, attached a bell to his collar so that everyone might know his malice and avoid him. But the dog, not knowing why his master had done this, believed that the bell was fastened to his collar as an honor and decoration, and so he began to despise all the other dogs. An old dog, knowing this and seeing him so proud and haughty, reprehended him saying: "Oh ill-fortuned fool, how mad and ignorant you are. You think that the bell on your neck, which was placed there to dishonor and reprehend you, is worn in honor and praise, for which reason you scorn and stand against the rest! Certainly you are publicly deceived. This bell is a witness to your malice which made you bite men. Know that for this reason you are adorned, so that people may guard against your manner and astute treachery. If you look in your heart, in no way are you raised above the rest of us." Hearing these words and turning away in great astonishment, red with guilty shame, the evil dog left the company.

Fable 7. Of the Camel and Jupiter

The wise man should content himself with what nature has given him and not covet the goods of others so that fortune may not go against him and take away what he has. For this reason, hear this fable. The camel, coming to the fields and seeing there a great herd of horned bulls, suffered grievously and complained, for he was not satisfied with what nature had given him. So, going to Jupiter, he began to lament: "Oh, what a shameful thing it is that a beast with a large body like mine should go without armor and protection. Bulls are armed with horns, boars with tusks, and even hedgehogs have their spines, and thus every animal according to his station. I alone am without arms and all the animals mock and ridicule me. Therefore, O Jupiter, most sovereign of all the gods, I beg that you give me horns like the bulls with which I can defend myself and not be scorned by all the other animals." Perceiving that the camel belittled the greatness he had already received, Jupiter took away almost entirely his large and beautiful ears. Smiling, Jupiter said: "Because you were not content with the things that nature and fortune gave you, I take away these ears so that you may always remember this correction, and so in fear and groaning you may spend your life." This fable warns that no one should covet another person's goods lest he lose what he formerly possessed quietly.

Fable 8. Of the Two Companions

This fable warns that we should not mingle in the company of unknown persons, especially those who have once been found to cheat and fraud. Two companions were traveling together through woods and valleys and down roads both level and rough in such unity and concord that they promised to help each other in any great or adverse fortune that should come upon them. They had barely finished expressing their offers when a bear appeared and came right toward them. Seeing this, the quicker of the two began to run away as fast as he could, and he climbed a tree. The other, knowing that he could not escape by climbing, stretched himself out on the ground as if dead, and he neither breathed nor moved. The bear turned him over from one side to the other, bringing his muzzle close to the man's mouth and ear while the man held his breath and did not move any part of his body. The bear thought the man was dead and lifeless because his limbs were cold and the natural warmth had departed from his bones because of his great fear. The bear even thought this was a putrefied body, and because it is not his nature to eat such meat, the bear let the man lie without hurting him and returned to his cave. After the bear had gone, the other man came down from his tree and said to his comrade: "I beg you to tell me what secret things the bear whispered in your ear when you were for so long placed in such great agony and fear of death." The man replied: "Certainly he taught me many different doctrines, most especially one that I was to commit to memory, and it is this: that insofar as I could, I should stay away from bad company and that whenever I should once feel myself cheated, thenceforth I should never be with him nor enter into his company again." These words said, he left his companion and went alone on his way, saying that it was better to go alone than ill accompanied.

Fable 9. Of the Two Pots

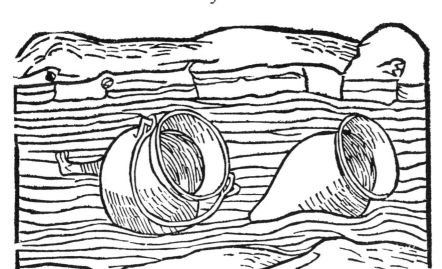

The poorest and lowest of men should not keep company with the rich and powerful, as this fable teaches us. When a river rose rapidly, it seized two pots that were on the bank and carried them away, one after the other. One pot was of copper and the other of clay. Their movement in the river was not equal because the earthen one, since it was lighter, went ahead and the copper one, being heavier, went behind. The copper pot, swearing not to do the clay pot any damage, asked the one ahead to wait for him so that they might go together. But the clay pot, knowing that a heavy object does harm to a lighter one and that one cannot make good company between the great and the small, replied: "Though you assure me with words, I cannot free my heart of fear. For if the waves make me touch you or you touch me, I shall always be in danger and subject to you and to the water and all the damage will come upon me. Thus your company is not good for me." This means that it is not suitable for the poor to keep company with the more powerful since all the profit of common good has to be toward the greater and the damage and travail to the poorer.

Fable 10. Of the Lion, the Bull, and the Goat

Anyone who receives injury or harm from someone should not avenge himself at a time when he is himself in danger of receiving a greater damage and injury. Instead he ought to wait for a time when he can take vengeance with profit, as this fable teaches us. The lion, who was going about looking for food, found a large bull grazing in a meadow, and as the bull saw the lion approaching him, he began to run away on rough roads and through unplowed fields toward the woods, trying to find a place to hide. Finally reaching a cave where a goat lived, the bull wished to hide himself in it. The goat, seeing that the bull wanted to come in, lowered his head and raised his horns so that he might not enter. The bull saw this, but for fear of the lion, he went his way without avenging himself on the goat, saying: "Now I suffer this injury and do not take vengeance on you, but do not believe it was for fear of you. Rather, I fear the lion which pursues me. If I did not fear him or if he were to go away, I would show you, you stinking, dirty, bearded goat, what difference there is between the strength of a bull and that of a goat; but because I am faced with a greater difficulty and danger, I do not now care for vengeance until I can execute it without danger." This fable signifies that it is sometimes better to suffer damage or injury so that when we wish to avenge ourselves, some other and greater injury may not overtake us.

Fable 11. Of the Ape and Her Son

Praise in one's own mouth soils and makes one vile, but each person likes his own qualities although they be more vile than those of others, concerning which this fable is told. One time, Jupiter, the greatest of the gods, desired to know which of all the animals he had created had the most beautiful offspring, so he ordered all the beasts, birds, and fish to present themselves before him with their young. Complying with his command, all the mothers of all the species of animals, birds, fish, and wild beasts came before Jupiter. Among them was a female ape with her son, who was more deformed and ugly than all the others before him. She presented him ahead of the rest and spoke most loftily: "O Jupiter, you know that I am winner in this, although one may perhaps believe differently concerning her own children. But according to my judgment, I say that my son is the most beautiful in form and build of all those present." Having heard the ape's words, Jupiter and all the company with him started to laugh quite heartily, and Jupiter said: "Do not try to praise your own, unless it has first been proven by a worthy testimony. And if you do not obey this injunction, you will always be scorned and mocked by all." This fable signifies that many men exalt what is their own more than that of others, although their own property may be vile and worthless.

Fable 12. Of the Crane and the Peacock

No one, although he has virtue and excellence greater than that of another person, should despise and scorn others, for although the others may lack something, they may yet have something better, as this fable demonstrates. The peacock asked the crane to have dinner with him, and when they were together to dine, in their conversation they began to discuss the virtues and natural gifts with which each was endowed. The peacock began to praise and exalt his plumage, which was varied and bright like a mirror; spreading and raising his tail over the crane, he said: "Observe so that you may contemplate my beauty and note how much it exceeds yours. See how your body and your feathers lack any shining color and are gray and without an agreeable appearance." Then the crane replied: "I recognize and I do not contradict the fact that the beauty of your feathers exceeds mine, but although nature has given those to you, more beautiful and more excellent than mine, for all that you still cannot fly up in the air; instead you are confined to the ground. Your feathers are not sufficient to raise you up and sustain you, while mine, although they do not shine and are dull and ugly, are sufficient to raise me and hold me in the air so that I may contemplate the marvels of this world with happiness in my heart, while you and your pride remain on the earth. Therefore, you ought not to scorn anyone because God has given you beauty, since you do not know with what virtues He has endowed others."

Fable 13. Of the Animal Called the Tigride*

The hidden whispering and secret detraction of the false tongue wounds more than an arrow, this fable teaches us. A hunter was so expert and clever in the art of the crossbow that rarely did his arrows miss their mark; as a result, all the animals feared him and did not dare to walk through the woods. But the animal called the tigride, seeing this, thought of a way that he might help to free the other animals from this danger. He said to them: "Do not be afraid, for I will help you and defend you with my strength, and no one need fear because I shall free you from all perils." As the animals were discussing these things, the hunter was hidden very close by. Hearing their talk, he made ready his crossbow and wounded the trigride most grievously, saying: "This my messenger I send to you to tell you who I am." While the tigride tried to draw out the arrow, a vixen came to him and said: "I beg you to tell me who it was that wounded you and where the arrow was hidden that has wounded you." The tigride, in great wrath and not able to speak perfectly because of the pain, groaned and sighed and spoke as best he could: "I looked this way and that and I looked behind, and I saw nothing to fear, but the blood that was spilled and the arrow by which I have been wounded show me that someone was hidden and that he is the one who wounded me. From this I can see how seriously hidden darts or arrows can wound." This means that every one should fear false and evil men who indulge in detraction and murmur falsely, because their evil words fly without hindrance like arrows of the crossbow, and they wound more ruthlessly than darts or arrows.

*A fantastic creature.

Fable 14. Of the Four Oxen

This fable teaches us that we ought not to believe false and flattering words nor give faith to flatterers and that we should not part from old company lightly. Four large and strong oxen had a friendship among themselves cemented with great treaties and oaths. They went all the time to pasture in the meadows, and so great was their friendship that they went to graze together without fear. They came and went, defending each other without danger or mishap, so that even when the hungry wolf came among them, they defended themselves with their horns, and they made the wolf flee in fear from their great harmony.

The wolf, seeing that his forces were not sufficient against the combined strength of the four and that no action would do him any good, considered how by trickery, falseness, and flattery he might separate each from the group so that he might kill them one by one. He approached them separately, telling each one how beautiful and strong he was, how he was abhorred by all the rest, and even that the others wished to persecute him. The wolf told each ox that he should look after himself and keep himself away from evil company which would soon fail him. The oxen were each suborned and deceived by the wolf, and when they gathered together, each one looked warily at the rest. Each considered how the others might harm him. Believing the words of the wolf, the oxen grew increasingly suspicious of one another and their friendship began to suffer. They no longer protected each other, but rather they went alone to pasture. The wolf, knowing that they were in discord and no longer grazed together, saw that his forces would be sufficient against each one of them and he killed separately the oxen whom he could not attack together and had previously feared. As the wolf reached the fourth and last bull, the bull spoke this warning to all animals: "He who wants to have a safe life, let him be advised by the deaths of the four of us that he should not heed flattery and deceitful words or forgo friendship and old companions. If we had remained in harmony, the wolf would not have attacked and eaten us."

Fable 15. Of the Pine Tree and the Turkey Oak or Blackthorn

One should not exalt himself because of his beauty or scorn others and sneer at them; frequently the most beautiful may fall while the ugly and deformed escape and remain unmolested, as this fable shows us. A very beautiful pine of marvelous stature near a turkey oak, or blackthorn, scornfully said: "How rough you are and without form and symmetry. You are not worthy to be near me. You ought not to share anything with me. My body is lofty, tall, and so straight that it almost reaches the clouds; my height extends to the stars, and I even have the central place in the big ships. They fasten sails to me to catch the wind and make the ship move and to guide the ship on the sea. In addition to these, I have innumerable virtues which you lack, and you are dull, ugly, and scorned and ridiculed by those who look upon you." But the turkey oak answered humbly: "Up to now you have been content with your beauty and belittled all of us for our ugliness, but they will cut your branches and trunk with the axe and you will be trimmed. Then how much more would my thorns please you than your branches, in which you are now rejoicing? For one should not presume himself better because of his good looks, for oftimes beauty leads to sadness and sighs, while the deformed and ugly live in peace and safety."

Fable 16. Of the Fisherman and the Little Fish

Man should not leave what he safely and peacefully possesses for something yet to come, for it may happen that he will seek and not find anything, as this fable tells. A fisherman on the shore of the sea caught a little fish, and as he was taking the hook from its mouth, the little fish said with a great sigh: "I ask you to take pity on me and let me go, as you see that you can get but little profit from me, since I am very small and was just born. No harm will come to you from this, and when I am big and fat, I will return to this shore and let myself be taken by you so that you and all your company can feed upon me." But the fisherman answered: "It would certainly be great madness to release a fish that has been caught and then work to catch another. No one should let go of what he has won with labor since there may later come a time when he would like to catch his prize but could not find it." And thus we should not leave what is certain for the uncertain; as the proverb says, a bird in the hand is worth more than a vulture on the wing.

Fable 17. Of the Sun and the Avaricious and Envious Man

So great is the envy of some persons that they actually wish to endure harm so that others might suffer greater discomforts, as this fable tells. Sovereign Jupiter sent someone from his lofty throne to the sun to find out the unscrupulous wishes of men. At that time two persons came before the sun: one was avaricious, the other envious. To them the sun said: "What would you like to ask for? Declare it in the knowledge that what you ask for first will be granted. The second thing you ask for will be doubled and given." Hearing this, the avaricious man wanted the envious to ask first so that the avaricious man himself might have the same thing doubled, since he thought that the envious one would ask for riches. The envious one, hearing this and considering what the avaricious man was to receive doubled, was not able to restrain his envy, and so he asked that he have an eye taken out, because then they would take two from the other man. The sun, seeing this, smiled at both and went up to Jupiter and told him to what extent envy reigned among men: many wished to expose themselves to dangers so that their neighbors might endure greater evils and harm. What joy it gives to the petty and tarnished to have companions in their ills and misfortunes!

Fable 18. Of the Weeping Lad and the Thief

They who covet the goods of others sometimes lose their own and do not recover them, as the present fable demonstrates. One time a lad, being near

a deep well, pretended to weep and so shed tears of feigned grief. Seeing this, a clever thief diligently inquired the cause of his grief, saying to him: "Tell me, handsome boy, why are you weeping so hard?" The boy answered sobbing: "I came here with a gold pot to fetch water, and as I was getting the water out the rope broke and so the pot fell into the well, and for this reason I grieve and weep." Hearing these words, the clever thief took off his cape, placing it near the boy, and went down into the well to seek the pot. As the thief entered and descended, the boy took his cape, fled to the woods, and hid there. The thief took a long time, as he was trying to find the gold pot, but realizing that he could not have it since it was not in the well and that he was wasting his time, he came out of the well and started looking everywhere for his cape, which he did not find. Lying on the ground, full of sadness and anguish, he said: "Oh gods of all people, what equal justice you have rendered. For with great reason those who are guided by envy and greed lose their cloaks, believing, that they will find the pot of gold in the well as I did." This fable warns that we should not be covetous and desire other men's goods, so that we may not lose our own property in seeking that of others and so it may not be said of us: "Fortunate is he whom the perils of others renders cautious and wise."

Fable 19. Of the Lion and the She-Goat

This fable shows us that we should not believe deceitful words. Looking over a field to see if perchance he sniffed some game, a hungry lion saw a she-goat grazing on a lofty crag. He wanted to eat her but could not climb up to the

crag. He spoke the following soft, deceptive words: "Tell me, sister, why do you dwell in these dry and unproductive places and try to eat on these lofty crags? Leave this uncultivated, empty, and sterile land. Descend into the green meadows where you will find many good herbs of various species and flowers which will give you joy." Sighing, the goat thought this was very good advice, but the natural enmity and antipathy between the two caused her to believe that the lion was misleading her. So the goat said: "I beg you not to reason any further in this way, for although all your words were true, your counsel is false. You're trying to deceive me with praise, a sweet voice, and pretty words which, if I believed them, would cause my death. Therefore go away, since it is safer for me to dwell here without fear than to follow your advice and come down to the meadows where I can be eaten." This fable shows us that we should not believe deceitful words, even though they might seem true. Rather, we should diligently consider to what end, in what manner, and by whom the words are spoken.

Fable 20. Of the Thirsty Crow

This fable teaches us that prudence and industry often take the place of strength. A very thirsty crow came to a well where he found a pail with such a small quantity of water in the bottom that he could not drink from it except by overturning it. As the pail was heavy, the crow's strength was not sufficient to move it. Impatiently thinking of various tricks he could use to satisfy the thirst that was almost killing him, the crow seized some stones in

his mouth and threw them into the pail. This raised the level of the water, and so the crow found a way to drink and put an end to his thirst. This fable signifies that through skill and cleverness one can accomplish many things which through force he cannot.

Fable 21. Of the Rustic and the Young Bull

One can hardly use words to castigate those who are of a rebellious and evil nature, as this parable demonstrates. A farmer began to yoke his new ox, who was rough and untamed, with a tame bull. The young ox, feeling the yoke over his head, began to rear up, throwing off the yoke and the straps, and then he tried to wound all those around him with his horns. Seeing this wildness, the farmer put restraints on his fore and hind feet and even cut off his horns, thinking that this would tame the ox and prevent him from doing further damage. Finally he put the yoke upon him again and tried to make him work. The young ox kicked and stamped and pawed the earth with his feet so that he threw dust and sand into his master's eyes. The master, in great anger, said: "I surely admit myself defeated by this bull, for his meanness is such that neither words nor blows can correct his behavior. But in a short while the butcher will punish him." This fable means that men of ill nature and upbringing are like wild bulls; they can never be punished with discipline or words, and justice is done only when they are hanged.

Fable 22. Of the Satyr and the Traveler

This fable demonstrates that men of forked tongues are to be shunned and avoided. A pilgrim, walking in distant and isolated regions where there raged the snow, rain, and freezing winds of a winter storm, reached a woods where there was so much snow and cruel wind that he could not see the road and did not know which way to turn. A satyr happened to see the pilgrim in this condition. Satyrs, men of small stature who live in the Atlas mountains of Libya, have small horns on their forehead and goat-like feet. This satyr, taking pity on the pilgrim, took him into his house. He was amazed by the great strength of the pilgrim, who, blowing on his cold hands, heated them and returned them to their natural state. After the pilgrim had warmed his hands, the satyr had him seat himself and gave the pilgrim the best food he had, and soon afterwards brought him a glass of hot wine so that he might warm himself inside. As the traveler brought the wine to his mouth, he noticed that it was very hot, and so, as before, he blew with his mouth to cool it. When the satyr saw this, he said: "I have seen you accomplish diverse things with the same mouth, because you can heat cold things and cool hot things. Go out of this wilderness and do not come back here again." Contrary operations of the mouth and the forked tongue are not to be tolerated anywhere. Those who praise and flatter those present and revile the absent must all the more be shunned. A two-faced person, who curses on one hand and makes peace on the other, is no laughing matter.

Fable 23. Of the Bull and the Mouse

The rule of the rich and powerful goes little farther than the degree to which they conform to the will of their subjects, as this fable tells. A big, strong bull, put out to exercise his limbs, was bitten repeatedly by a little mouse with tiny teeth. The bull turned this way and that to get rid of the rodent. The mouse fled to a hole but soon returned to the bull again. He did this so many times that the bull became very angry. Although he was strong and robust, the bull could not avenge himself because he could scarcely see the mouse. The mouse tolerated the bull's anger with patience because he knew that he was safe from him. The mouse then spoke these words to the bull: "Although nature has given you a large body, you cannot do me any harm. Even though I am small of body, I trouble you who are large, and you cannot avenge yourself upon me. Through my words you may learn your own strength: conform yourself with the will of your subjects and scorn no one, and thus you will be able to use your power and strength freely." This means that the powerful ought to get along with their subjects and not scorn them, however small they may be, if they wish to maintain their estate and honor.

Fable 24. Of the Goose and Its Master

Whoever has enough to suffice him but is not content with it ought justly to lose what he has, according to this fable. A man had a goose which laid a golden egg in her nest each day, but the man soon became discontented with this and desired the goose to lay two each day. The goose, who was unable to satisfy her lord's greed no matter how much she tried, laid her egg as she was accustomed to do. But the man, thinking about the origins of this golden egg, believed that the goose had some treasure hidden inside her from which she derived her egg. Then, so that he might take all the treasure at once, the greedy man killed the goose, opened up her insides, and looked everywhere for the treasure. He lost all hope because he had found nothing and because the goose had died. He recognized his greed and thought about his foolish actions, and with sighs and groans he bore his pain and misfortune. For it was just that since he was rich and had looked for more, he lost what he had started with. Therefore, it is fitting for everyone to be content with what God has given him and not to think small what is reasonable for him. He should thank God for what he has rather than lose it in order to reach for other and greater things.

Fable 25. Of the Ape and Her Two Sons

Sometimes it happens that things that we despise and think to be of little value become beloved by us and, on the contrary, things that we love the most are lost and left unprotected, as this fable tells. Once upon a time a female ape bore two sons together which she did not raise in equal fashion. By natural inclination she loved one more than the other, and she continually praised and tried to please that son. She hated the other and did him no good nor did she praise him, save what by a natural mother's love she could not deny him. She gave him only enough so that he might subsist. It happened that the ape, going through the woods with her two sons, heard some hunters and their dogs. She became fearful and thought of how she might escape without harm. She took the son she loved best in her arms, embraced him tenderly, and then made the son she hated climb up on her back. In this way she fled as best she could. But the dogs followed and pressed her, and wanting to avoid the death of the son she had in her arms, she wished to throw off the son whom she had on her back. However, he held very tightly to his mother's neck and he escaped with her without harm from the dogs. When the ape lost the son she loved the most, she began to love the other and gave him all the kindness that she had given to the first so that he was the sole heir to the goods of both father and mother. This means that sometimes fortune makes one who was scorned more loved than the one who in another time was more beloved and appreciated.

Fable 26. Of the Storm and the Pot

Certainly he is unfortunate who cannot escape from the scandals and dangers of this world. Through pride or vainglory, this man believes himself greater than his estate requires, as this story shows and as we can see by common experience. A potter once made a pot, putting much of his knowledge and art into its making. So that it might bake in the best fashion, he left it out to dry in the air. At this same time, there arose a great storm with wind and rain; when the storm reached the pot, it asked: "What are you? And what name do you have?" And the pot, not remembering what it was and forgetting that it was made of earth and soft clay, replied: "I am a pot. I have been made by the skill of my master and by his well-practiced hand, and I was formed by continual turning so that I remain a pot of good composition." The storm then replied: "Although you think yourself a well-formed pot, know that in a little while you will return to what you were; soaked by this water, you will realize that you are nothing but soft earth and water." And having said these words, the storm poured a quantity of water upon the pot. As the pot was made of clay and water and had not yet been baked in the furnace, it went back to being clay and water. This fable teaches that each of us ought to see ourselves accurately and not to think ourselves more than we are. What an easy thing it is to consider ourselves noble, generous, and important, but it is difficult to maintain nobility and value. To write more on this matter would evoke criticism and envy; therefore I cease to go on.

Fable 27. Of the Wolf and the Kid

Although all things have an inclination toward good, reason may present the will with two evils. The lesser is to be chosen, as this story declares. A little goat was grazing in a field not far from his home when a wolf saw him and came to eat him. When he saw the wolf, the goat began to flee, running toward home where the cattle were. The wolf, seeing that he could not capture the goat by force, thought to tempt him with soft words, saying: "O foolish animal lacking foresight, what do you seek in this place among the cattle? Perhaps do you not notice how everywhere in the temple the ground is wet with the blood of these creatures that are every day sacrificed to the gods? I beg you not to stay here where you can hope for nothing except death. Return to the meadow where you can live without danger and fear." The goat answered the wolf: "I beg you, my lord, not to concern yourself in this business, for neither by your insistence nor by your bad counsel will you be able to make me leave here, even though I must continually fear death. It is better to endure all this and be sacrificed to the gods than to be eaten by a ravenous wolf." This means that of two present evils, one should choose the lesser.

VIII. The Collected Fables of Alfonso, of Poggio, and of Others

Here begin the Collected Fables of Alfonso and of Poggio and of others in the form and order which follow:

Fable 1. In Which Alfonso Advises People about Wisdom and True Friendship

The wise Lucania* of Arabia said to his son: "You ought not believe that the ant, which stores in summer what it will live on in winter, is wiser than you.

*Lucania, erroneous spelling of Lucaman, the eastern sage who is credited with collecting many fables.

Let not the rooster be a better watchman than you, for he keeps guard in the morning while you sleep. Do not let the one who rules nine wives be stronger than you because you cannot rule even one. Do not let the dog, who always remembers the kindnesses he receives, be more noble in heart than you who do not remember. Do not underestimate an enemy, however small he may be, and let it not seem much to you to have a thousand friends."

Later, the same Arabian sage was at the point of death, called his son and asked him how many friends he had acquired up to that day.

The son replied: "According to what I think, I have one hundred friends."

The father said: "Consider no one a friend until you have tested him. I was born before you and scarcely do I have one half-friend, and even this one was gained with a great deal of labor. It surprises me that you could have so many friends. You ought to test them so that you may know in truth which of them are your friends."

The son replied: "Father, how should I test them?"

The father said: "Test them in this way: kill a calf, put it in a sack, and let the sack be bloodied on the outside. Carry it to a friend of yours and tell him that it is a dead man who you killed by accident. Say that you are begging him, as a special friend, to hide and bury the body so that your crime will not be known, since he can do so without suspicion. Tell him that through his friendship you can escape this danger."

The son took his father's advice. He went to a friend with the corpse and beseeched him according to his father's suggestion. The friend replied: "Take your dead man on your back. Don't come into my house with him. If you committed the crime, you suffer the punishment."

Afterwards, he took the corpse to his other friends, begging them one after another with the same words. They all replied in the same way, saying: "The case is serious and dangerous, and therefore it isn't fitting that you enter our houses with such a thing as that. Decide for yourself how you will manage. You committed the crime; don't put us into danger."

The son, seeing his friends' shallow loyalty, returned to his father and told him all that had happened. The father said: "Now you have truly acted like the philosopher who says, "Many are friends in name, but few indeed are found in time of need. Now go to my half-friend, test him, and see how he will react."

The son went to the friend as his father advised, and told him that he carried a dead man. The friend said to him: "Come into the house, for this secret must not be revealed to the neighbors." Then he had his wife and all the household leave the house, and he secretly dug in the most convenient place in the house to bury that corpse. Thus when the friend was to bury the body the son revealed the entire matter truthfully to him. The son thanked the man profusely and then returned to tell his father all the deeds and words of his half-friend. The father said: "The philosopher says about such a friend: "The one who helps you when every one fails you is a good friend."

The son asked his father: "By chance have you seen any one who was a whole friend?"

The father replied: "I never saw one, but I've heard of one."

The son begged him: "Tell me if I shall ever be able to find such a whole friend."

"The story I heard was about two merchants, one of whom was in Egypt, the other lived in Baldac, and they knew one another only by hearsay, messages, and the letters they sent to one another that acted as contracts for selling, buying, and other diverse matters. As time went by, it happened that the merchant from Baldac went to do business in Egypt. The Egyptian, hearing that his friend was coming, went out to meet him with great joy, and then received him in his house, and served him, as is customary among friends, for seven days, all the while showing him his goods, riches, and secrets. This done, the man from Baldac began to feel ill. Feeling sorry for his friend, the Egyptian merchant sought all the doctors in the province, and choosing the best among them had them come to his house to cure his friend. But the doctors, having taken his pulse and having seen his urine, found no bodily disease and determined that he was grieving in his mind and soul. His sickness was a flame of love and desire.

"Learning this, the Egyptian went to him and asked him whether in his house there was any woman whose love had thus enflamed him and made him ill. The sick man replied: 'Show me all the women in your house. If I see among them the one whom my fancy loves so greatly, I will tell you the truth.' Then the Egyptian brought before him all the women and servant girls in the house, but he was not pleased by any of them. He then brought forward his daughters, but the sick man did not choose any one of them. There was also in the house a maiden with a large dowry who had been living with the merchant for a long time so that she might learn his ways and eventually become his wife. She was finally brought to the sick man, and when he saw her he said: 'Upon this girl depends my life or death.' Hearing these words, the Egyptian without delay gave the girl to his friend for a wife. She was noble, and beautiful and had a large dowry, and the Egyptian himself had intended to have her for his own wife. And so, the friend grew well and, his business concluded, he returned to his country with his wife.

"Some time later it happened that the merchant of Egypt lost all his wealth through various unfortunate occurrences. Thus, having fallen into poverty, he decided to go and visit his friend in Baldac so that he might have pity on him and help him. The Egyptian set out, ill-clad and hungry, and reached Baldac at night, but he was ashamed to go to his friend's house at that time. Since he was half naked and unclean, he also feared to go at that hour, as his friend might not recognize him. For this reason, he decided to enter the temple and pass the night there.

"As he began to ponder many things, being in the temple started to irritate him, so he went out in order to rid himself of those thoughts. On leaving the temple, he encountered two men in the street and saw one of them kill the other and flee, hiding himself in the city. The citizens, hearing the noise and the blows, came out to see what was going on. They found the dead man and looked everywhere for the murderer, but they met no one other than the Egyptian, who they took and asked if he had killed that man. Having fallen into poverty and desiring that his ill fortune should be concluded, he answered: 'I killed him.' He was taken and put in prison that night, and the following day he was taken before the judges and sentenced to be hanged. As is the custom, many people went to see justice done in the place where the Egyptian was to be hanged. Among them was his friend of Baldac, on whose account the accused had come to that city. When he saw the Egyptian and looked more carefully, the merchant recognized him as the Egyptian from whom he had received much honor, his wife with a large dowry, and many other benefits and goods. Remembering all that and considering that a man is obliged to give thanks to a friend for benefits received in his life, since one cannot pay these things back after death, he decided to take his friend's place. He began to cry out in a loud voice: 'O evil judges, why do you condemn someone who has no guilt? This one you wish to kill is innocent and does not deserve death; I am the one who deserves the penalty because I killed the man he claims to have killed.' Hearing these words, the judges had him seized and condemned to death, while they released the Egyptian.

"The true killer, seeing all these things, contemplated the crime he had committed and considered the love and faith of the two friends and how the one wished so kindly for the other not to die. He concluded that it was just that he, being guilty, should die instead of the innocent friends. He began to cry out loudly, saying: 'Listen, executors of justice, truly God is a just judge who leaves no evil nor crime unpunished. So that God may not order my crime punished more severely in the next world, I confess that I am the true murderer, and I am ready to suffer the penalty for the crime that I committed. Therefore, free this man who is not guilty and condemn me instead.'

"The judges marveled and had him seized. Wondering how they should judge the case, they sent the three men to the king to tell him all that had happened, but the king was no less perplexed by the case. Finally, all the learned men decided that since the murderer had confessed freely, he should be pardoned. Thus all three men were freed, and each was able to overcome the desire to die.

"They all went their ways in peace. The merchant of Baldac took the Egyptian to his house, and seeing his poverty and want, comforted him in this manner: 'If you wish to join my company all the things that I possess are yours as well as mine, and if you so wish, let us divide all that I possess in equal parts. You take one part, and I shall be content with the other.'

"The merchant from Egypt, from love for the land of his birth, received the part of the goods that his friend gave him and departed for his own country."

All these things having been told, the son said to his father: "Such a friend as that I never expect to have."

Fable 2. Of the Cash Held in Trust

A Spaniard, going to Mecca, arrived in Egypt and realized that he must soon pass through sparsely populated and desert regions. Fearing robbery and the dangers of the road, he decided to leave the money he would not need for his trip with a trusted man in Egypt. Everyone believed that the Egyptian man was loyal, of good faith, and of great excellence, and so the traveler entrusted him with twenty silver marks. He went to Mecca and completed his business, and upon his return to Egypt he demanded his silver of the man to whom he had entrusted it.

The guardian, being full of guile, denied the deposit and said that he had never even seen such a man. Hearing this, the Spaniard went sadly to the companions with whom he had come and asked their advice about the deposit of silver he had been denied by the good man.

The neighbors and his companions did not believe him, saying that the man was kind, virtuous, and very truthful and that he would not do such a thing. Hearing his friends' praise of the man, the Spaniard went to him again with great humility and respect, thinking that he would thus induce him to return the silver. However, the more the deceiver was asked the more he denied, and he threatened and reviled the Spaniard because he had defamed him. The Spaniard again turned away sadly.

He met an old lady who was dressed in a nun's habit and walked with a staff. This old lady, seeing the disturbed and groaning foreigner, was moved by pity and asked him what was the matter and why was he so distressed. He told her the whole story of what had happened with the loyal and reputable man. The good old woman began to encourage him, saying that if what he said was true, with the help of God there was hope of recovering the loss. The Spaniard asked her how that might be, and she answered: "Bring me a man from your country whom you trust."

He brought her a companion, and the old lady told him to make four caskets with painted surfaces, well built and decorated with gold and silk. He should then fill them with little stones and have them carried by some men to the house of the man who denied possession of the silver. They should be brought one at a time so that the Egyptian would believe that the traveler wished to leave them in his care to be guarded. "And when these men go into the house with those four caskets, you will go in and demand your silver, which God willing, you will get."

The Spaniard went and ordered all the things exactly as the old woman had advised. As he, his companion, and the old woman entered with those caskets into the house of he who had denied the deposit, they told the deceiver: "Sir, here are some Spanish merchants who bring treasures of precious stones, gold, and silver. They want to go to Mecca, and having heard of your honesty, loyalty, and diligence, they ask you to keep these four caskets until their return, for they do not dare take them for fear of being robbed in the desert. No less do we ask than that, out of respect for us, you will honor this request: that this remain a secret among us because they are men who do not wish anyone to know of the great treasure they are carrying." While they were telling this tale and carrying the chest up to a room, the first Spaniard came with confidence to claim his silver, as the old lady had told him to do. The keeper who had denied the money saw the Spaniard and feared that he would tell a bad tale to those who were bringing the caskets or that he might complain in front of them, and so he said: "Friend, why have you delayed so long in requesting the silver that I have on deposit for you? I am tired of keeping it so long."

He ordered it to be given to the Spaniard because he feared that if he denied he had received it to guard, then the chests full of treasure would not be entrusted to him. As the company saw that the man had returned the Spaniard's silver, the men did not trouble to come back for the chests filled with stones. So, by another trick, the Spaniard got his money back.

Fable 3. Of the Subtle Artifice of Wisdom in Enigmatic Casks of Oil Held in Trust

At his death, a man left his son nothing but a house. The son, seeking to earn his poor living with his hands, often suffered from hunger, but in memory of his father he bore the lack of resources and labor rather than sell the house. A rich and greedy neighbor of his sought to possess the house and have it for his own, and so he set in motion many plots against the lad. The son realized this and avoided the man's company as much as he could so that he would not be deceived by the crafty man.

The rich man, knowing that the son did not wish to sell him the house, came to him with sweet words saying that since he did not wish to sell him his house, a virtuous action, he should at least rent a portion of it to store ten casks of oil. The man said the son would profit by this and have no damage whatsoever. Induced by these words, the lad rented the man a room, even though he did it against his will, because he did not think that he would be cheated. As the lad went to negotiate what he had agreed to do, the rich man had the earth dug up and deposited there five casks of oil and in another place five half casks. So, when the man came, he received from the lad the keys to the room with the casks and said: "Good youth, I entrust my casks and oil to your guardianship." And so he went away, bidding him farewell. The young man, not suspecting any trickery, believed that all the casks he had received into his custody were full.

A short while later, as oil was bringing a good price, the rich man said to the youth: "Let us sell the oil that is in your care. As is right, you will get the rent and reward for your labor." The lad went with him to see the buyers, and together they found five casks full of oil and five half full. Having seen this, the deceitful rich man said: "Friend, you have defrauded me in the keeping of my oil. I ask you to give it back and make good what is lacking." The youth denied that any fraud had taken place, but he was sent before a judge and accused of the crime. The boy answered the accusation saying that he did not deny having the casks of oil in his custody, but that he was not guilty of the crime of which he was accused, and he asked for time to defend his rights.

During the space of time allotted by the judge, the youth went and took the counsel of a philosopher, who was virtuous and a defender of the poor. He humbly asked him for aid and advice, declaring the whole matter to the philosopher and affirming by oath that he was unjustly accused. The philosopher, moved by pity and noting the purity and decency of the lad, said: "Son, be of good cheer, for I will help you. Truth should be preferred to deceit." So the next day the youth went to court with the philosopher, who was also established as an adviser of the council and of the king's court. As the arguments were heard for each side, the king said to the philosopher: "I commit this case to you, so that with a just sentence you may judge it." The philosopher, obeying the king's command, spoke as follows: "The rich man is of such good reputation that it cannot be thought that he would ask for what is not truly owed him. No less can it be presumed that this lad, who up to now has not been corrupted and is not of bad reputation, has stolen the oil. So that the truth may be discerned, let the oil and the dregs in the five full casks be measured and next let the oil and dregs of the half empty casks be measured as well. Then let it be seen whether the sediment in the half empty casks and in the full casks is of the same quantity. I think this will sufficiently prove the oil to have been stolen; however, if in the half full casks there is but one half of the sediment that was found in the full ones, then the accused should be freed."

And so it was found, that there was but half the amount of sediment in the half full casks that there was in the full ones. Thus, the lad was free of the rich man's false accusation by the philosopher's judgment. the lad gave thanks to the philosopher and then went home in peace.

Fable 4. Of the Artifice of the Missing Money

Going through a city, a rich merchant lost a small bag containing one thousand florins in the street. A poor man found it, carried it home, and gave it to his wife to keep. She said with joy: "Whatever happens to me, I shall never throw this away. If the Lord gave us these riches, let us keep them."

The next day it was announced throughout the city that a man had lost one thousand florins and that he promised one hundred florins as a reward to him who would return them. The man who found them said to his wife: "Let us return these thousand florins, and we will have one hundred without sin and weight on our conscience. These one hundred florins will profit us more than all those to which we have no claim."

Even though his wife wished to keep them, the husband returned the one thousand florins and asked for the reward of one hundred. But, when the rich man saw the thousand florins in his grasp, he said to the poor man: "You have not given back all that you found, for there are four hundred florins lacking. When you bring those back I will be ready to pay you your one hundred florins." The poor man maintained that he had found no more than the one thousand florins, and so the two men contending over this, went before the king, in whose power they placed the florins. The king commanded that the matter should be examined and judged by a philosopher who was called the helper of the poor. The petition was placed before the philosopher-judge who, moved by pity, said to the poor man: "Tell me the truth. Have you anything that belongs to this rich man? Or have you returned all that was his?" The poor man replied: "God knows that I returned all that I found."

Then the philosopher said: "This man is rich and creditable, and he brings much testimony in his favor. It is not to be believed that he would demand what he had not really lost, for he affirms under oath that he has lost fourteen hundred florins, and it is to be believed that he speaks the truth. This other man, although poor, is also of good reputation and should no less be believed. Furthermore, he has restored one thousand florins which he could have retained if he had wished to burden his soul, and he affirms with a strong oath that he has returned all that he found. Therefore, most high king, my judgment is that the following sentence be pronounced: these one thousand florins should be held on deposit, of which one hundred should be given to the poor man. For indeed it seems that these thousand florins are not the ones that this honorable man lost, since he swears that he lost fourteen hundred. The one thousand will be kept for whoever lost them, and if by chance anyone should find the fourteen hundred that this rich man says he lost, they will be returned to him."

This sentence pleased the king and all present, but upon hearing the judgment, the rich man repented his deceit and begged for the king's mercy, saying: "Oh great prince, have pity on me. I know my sin and the deceit that I practiced, and I wish to make the truth known. Certainly these one thousand florins are mine, but I wished to defraud this poor man in order not to give him the one hundred florins that I promised." The king, practicing clemency, ordered that the thousand florins should be returned to him, and of them one hundred given to the man who found them. Thus the poor man was freed of the rich man's false demand through the help of this good and just judge.

Fable 5. Of the Faith or Deceit of the Three Companions

Often a man falls into the trap that he sets for another, as is recounted in this fable. There were three companions who, because of their piety, were on a pilgrimage to the city of Mecca. Two were merchants and city men, and the third was a country man.

They all lacked food on the journey, and they had nothing to eat but a little flour which sufficed only to make a small loaf of bread. Perceiving this, the deceitful city men said to one another: "We have but little bread and our companion is a great eater. Therefore, we must think of how we may eat this small amount of bread without him." Having made the flour into dough and setting it to bake, the merchants tried to find a way to deceive the rustic. The merchants said: "Let us all go to sleep and the one among us who shall have the most wonderful dream shall eat the bread." Having agreed to this arrangement, they all went to sleep. The rustic, understanding his companions' trick, took out the half-baked bread, ate it alone, and went back to sleep.

A little while later, one of the merchants, as if startled by a dream, began to get up. One of his companions asked him: "Why are you startled?" He answered: "I am made afraid by a marvelous dream. It seemed to me that two angels, opening the gate of heaven, took me before the throne of the Lord God with great joy." His companion said: "That is a wonderful dream. But I saw something even more marvelous, for I saw two angels who took me from terra firma to hell." The rustic, hearing all this, pretended to sleep. But the two city dwellers wished to end their deceit, and they awoke the rustic cleverly, as if they were frightened. The rustic said: "Who are these who call me?" they replied: "We are your comrades." The rustic asked them: "How did you come back?" They answered: "We never left here. Why do you speak of our return?" The rustic said: "It seemed to me that two angels, opening the gates of heaven, took one of you before God and the other was dragged through the earth to hell. I thought that you would never come back here, and since I have never heard of anyone returning from paradise or from hell, I got up and ate the bread by myself." This fable shows that sometimes while thinking to deceive another ignorant man, the same type of fellow is himself deceived.

Fable 6. Of the Little Bird and the Countryman

A villager had a garden much ornamented by grass, flowers, and a clean running stream, all of which attracted many birds. One day he went, as he was accustomed to do, to rest in the garden. Feeling tired, he sat down beneath a tree in which a little bird was singing very sweetly. Hearing her delightful song, the rustic set up a snare and caught her. The bird, being thus captured, said: "Why did you take so much trouble to catch me since you can derive no profit from me?" The rustic answered: "I caught you because

your song delights my heart." The little bird replied: "You worked in vain, for I shall not sing for you, not by request or for a reward." The rustic said: "If you do not sing, I shall kill you and eat you." The bird replied: "In what manner will you eat me? Boiled in water, the mouthful will indeed be so small that you won't even notice me. If you bake me, I shall be even smaller. Let me fly and you will derive great profit from me because I will give you three doctrines of wisdom which you will enjoy more than three meals." And, as the bird promised these things, he set her free. She said to him: "Let this be the first teaching: do not believe all that you hear, especially those things that do not sound truthful. Secondly, keep what is yours, and thirdly and finally, do not to grieve over what you have lost and cannot recover."

These words concluded, the bird went up into a tree and sang her song very sweetly. "Blessed be the Lord God who blinded the good sense of this hunter and took away his prudence so that he might not touch me, look at me, or discover the precious stone called the jacinth, an ounce in weight, that I bear inside me. If he knew that I have such a thing I would die in his hands and he would become very rich." The rustic, hearing this, was deeply troubled because he had let the little bird go. In great grief he said: "Oh unlucky me, I believed the words of that deceitful bird and did not keep what I had!" To this she replied: "You are mad to torment yourself! Have you so quickly forgotten the advice that I gave you? Do you think that a little bird as small as I, who altogether does not weigh more than a drachma, which is as much as a coin, can carry in my insides an ounce of jacinth? Do you not remember what I told you? Do not believe all that you hear, and if I was yours, why did you not keep me? And if you lost the stone but cannot recover

it, why do you criticize the three doctrines that I gave you?" Having said
these things and having mocked the rustic, the little bird went her way.

Fable 7. Of the Rimester and the Humpback

A learned man said to his son: "If you are aggrieved in anything but can be in
some way relieved, do not enter into the question nor let it become enlarged.
Free yourself as quickly as possible so that another greater annoyance may
not come upon you, as this fable shows. A rimester presented an excellent
king with some verses containing praises and accounts of the king's great
deeds. The king, wishing to remunerate the rimester for his services, said to
him: "Ask what you like in the knowledge that it will be granted you." The
rimester asked the king to make him doorkeeper of his city for a month
under the following conditions: that whoever had a bodily defect and passed
through that gate should pay him one coin for each blemish, whether he be
itchy, scabby, ruptured, or having a defect of the eyes or any other body part.
The king, being very pleased with the verses, authorized all that the rimester requested and ordered that he be given his sealed document of privilege.

The rimester, taking up his new office of doorkeeper, was seated at the
gate when a humpback passed over the bridge and reached the gate. The
humpback, who was well covered by his cape and had a shepherd's crook in
his hand, wished to pass through the gate. The porter asked him for a coin,
saying that he was humpbacked. As the man did not wish to pay, the

rimester seized his cape and removed it. Looking more closely, he also saw that the man was blind in one eye. The rimester said to him: "You must pay two coins because you have only one eye and you did not want to pay one coin." The traveler was no less recalcitrant about paying two coins, so the porter pulled the cap off the man's head and discovered it was scabby. The porter said to the man: "You must pay three coins, for you are also scabby." The humpback did not wish to pay, so the porter tried to take three coins from him by force. The humpback, rolling up his sleeves to defend himself, revealed arms that were wrinkled and itchy, and so the porter said to him: "You must pay four coins." The porter, wanting to make the humpback pay the coins by virtue of his privilege, and the humpback, refusing to pay because the porter was doing him a wrong, came to blows.

As the humpback fell to the ground, the porter discovered a rupture and said: "You owe five coins, for you are also ruptured in addition to your other blemishes." So finally the humpback had to pay five coins because in the beginning he did not wish to pay one. Therefore, when you can avoid some danger by paying a small amount, do not hesitate to give the little to avoid arguments in which you might lose a great deal.

Fable 8. Of the Sheep

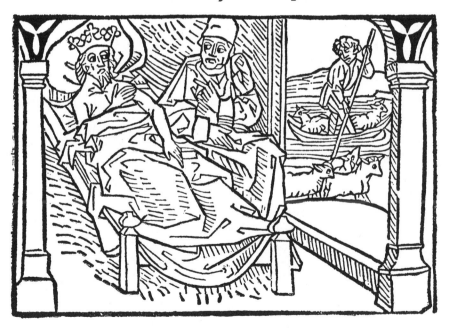

A disciple who greatly enjoyed hearing fables from his master asked him to tell him a long fable. The master replied: "Be careful lest there happen to us what befell a king with his teller of fables." The disciple said: "Good master, tell me how that was." The master told him the following: "A king had a fabulist, a writer of stories and fables who, every time the king wanted to relax, had to tell the king five fables which he might enjoy.

It happened that one night the king's imagination was so active that he could not sleep. For this reason, he ordered more than the usual five fables, and the fabulist told him three additional good ones. The king said: "These fables are all very well, but tell me one that is long, and after that you may go to sleep." So the fabulist began in this fashion: "There once was a villager who amassed a thousand coins with which he went to a fair and bought two thousand sheep. And, returning to his home with the sheep, he discovered that the river had risen to the point that he could not pass over it with his sheep, and he could pass neither by the bridge nor by the ford. He worried about how he would get his sheep over. Finally he found a boat in which he could pass over one sheep at a time, or two with great difficulty. And so he began to take the sheep over two by two," and, saying these words, the fabulist fell asleep.

The king woke him from his sleep and asked him to finish his story. He answered: "O great king, the river is wide and the boat is small, and the sheep almost without number and you, king of innumerable sheep, let the rustic and the sheep pass over. Then I will finish the story that I began." And with these pleasant words, the king, who was fond of fables, was content.

And so the master said to his disciple: "Son, if from now on you annoy me about many fables, I shall cause you to recall this fable so that you may be content with those that I shall tell."

Fable 9. Of the Wolf, the Rustic, the Fox, and the Cheese

One should not let a certain thing go in the hope of an uncertain one, as the wolf shows us. In the same way, a man should not entrust his affairs to the power of a false judge because false judges are easily corrupted, like the fox of which this fable speaks. There was a farmer who had some oxen that, with great difficulty, he made plow in a straight line. Many times he said: "May the wolves eat you, because you only walk crookedly!"

Hearing this, a wolf spent a whole day waiting for the farmer to give them to him, but as night came, the wolf saw that he had waited in vain because the farmer unhitched the oxen and sent them home. So the fox said to the farmer: "You have promised me the oxen many times this day. Fulfill your promise; I am ready to receive them." The farmer replied: "I only promised them in general terms and that does not oblige me, for I did not swear it with an oath." The wolf replied: "You shall not leave here until you fulfill the promise."

They argued at length about this, but they finally agreed that the

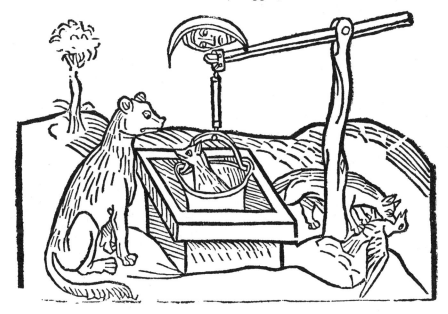

question should be decided by attorneys and judges of equal stature. As they were looking for their judges, they met a vixen who asked them: "Friends, where does your prosperous road lead you?" They then related the story in detail. She said to them: "For this you need no other judges, for I myself will judge between you very well. So that I may be better informed and make my determination of the question more briefly, I wish to speak with each one of you privately. If this pleases you, tell me so that you may not later have to go looking for another judge later." They answered that they were satisfied.

The vixen first began to talk with the farmer, to whom she said: "If you will give me a pair of chickens for me and my mate, I'll see to it that your oxen are safe and that you are free of your promise."

The farmer was content with this, and so the vixen said to the wolf: "Listen friend, I owe you a debt for the good deeds I have received from you in past times. I have worked with the farmer and have arranged that he is to give you a big cheese if you stop this lawsuit that you have against him on account of the oxen and if you leave him in peace." The wolf agreed to this and thanked the fox. The fox ordered the farmer to depart with his oxen, and she then said to the wolf: "You are to go with me and I will take you to a place where you will find the cheese in question." She led the wolf hither and thither through various places until the moon appeared.

When the moon had come up, the vixen took the wolf to a well where she pointed out the reflection of the moon in the water. She said to him: "Friend, look at the big, choice cheese. Go down and get it." The wolf replied: "Sister, you ought to give me the cheese. You go down, and if you cannot come up alone, I will help you."

Slyly, the vixen agreed to this. Attached to the well were two buckets tied with a rope, with which they drew water, so that when one bucket went down the other came up. The fox got into one of the buckets and went down into the well. She was there some time, and the wolf finally asked: "Friend, why do you take so long to bring up the cheese?" He suspected that the fox wished to eat the cheese. The fox replied: "It is so big that I cannot get it out alone. You must get into the other bucket and come down to help me." The wolf got into the other bucket and began to descend, but because he was heavier than the vixen, he made the other bucket with the vixen inside go up. As soon as she saw herself at the rim of the well, she joyfully jumped out and left the wolf down in the well. So because the wolf let go of a present benefit for an uncertain good to come and believed a false middleman, he lost both the oxen and the cheese. Therefore, do not seek to leave the certain for the uncertain, and do not place your affairs in the hands of bad judges or go-betweens.

Fable 10. Of the Young Wife and Her Husband, of the Mother-in-Law and the Adulterer

The deceits of women are innumerable, as the following fables prove. A merchant leaving for a fair left his wife in the care of his mother-in-law to keep the wife honest and chaste. But this merchant's wife, with the consent of her mother, dishonestly received a young man for a lover. To bind their relationship, the latter was invited to her lodging, and being thus together, the young man, the mother, and the daughter were eating with great pleasure. But here came the merchant back from the fair and knocked at the door. There was no place where the lad could flee or hide, and the woman was very anxious, not knowing what to do.

But the mother-in-law, who was an old trickster and wanted to quickly repair the damage, counseled the young man to have his sword drawn, to be facing the door where the husband was knocking, to show the young man's ferocity and belligerence, and not to give any answer whatsoever except by gestures. He was to act as if he wished to wound and hurt the one who was knocking at the door, and the young man carried out this maneuver as the old lady had counseled him.

Meanwhile, the woman pulled a rope which was fastened to the lock on the door and opened the postern gate shutter so that the husband could come in. He came by the postern and saw the man there with a naked sword in his hand. The husband stopped and said: "Who are you?" And the young man, answering nothing, caused even more fear. The mother-in-law said: "Quiet, my dear son." The merchant, marveling at this, said: "My dear lady mother, what is all this?" She answered: "Honored son, the matter is this: three men wished to kill this man at the door, and we let him come in here with his sword in hand. Because the door is open, he now thinks you are one of his attackers. Because he is afraid, he does not answer."

The merchant said: "Oh, how well you have done to help this man escape from death!" He boldly came in and greeted the lad, had him sit down with him, and talked to him in a friendly manner. The merchant sent him away in peace, considering him a friend henceforth.

Fable 11. Of the Old Lady Who Deceived the Chaste Woman with a Little Dog

It is told that a nobleman had a very chaste and beautiful wife. Wishing to go on a pilgrimage to visit the holy relics, he did not want to appoint another to guard his wife, trusting in her good habits. After her husband had gone, this woman lived chastely and honestly in all ways.

Returning from a certain business matter concerning her house, she was seen by a young man who at once began to fall in love with her. On days when she did not appear, he was beside himself. She was sought after by many of the young man's go-betweens and sent many jewels, but she was never willing to yield to his importunities. The young man saw that she totally despised him, and he felt such great anxiety and love that he fell ill. Sick as he was, he often went by the house of his beloved, looking very sad and grieving so that at times he shed tears.

While in this state, he met an old lady of decent appearance in the habit of a nun. She asked the cause of his sadness and weeping, but he did not wish to reveal his secret to the old lady. She said to him: "The sick man who does not wish to tell his illness to the physician endures more pain." He heard this and observed that she was a serious person, and so he told her of his affliction in detail and asked her advice. The old lady consoled him as follows: "Be comforted, for unless I am deceived, in a little while you will have the things that you desire." She went away, leaving him hopeful.

Returning to her house, the old lady shut up a little dog in a room and left her three days without food. She then made her eat a piece of bread soaked in mustard; as the hungry dog ate the bread, tears began to run from her eyes on account of the sharpness and bitterness of the mustard. The old woman led this weeping dog to the house of the chaste woman, who received the nun with a happy face and most honorable feeling, pleased at being called upon by the old woman, who was thought to be of good and religious life. As they were talking together, the chaste woman noticed how the little dog was weeping, and she asked the cause of its tears. The old lady, sharpening her wits, said: "O well beloved friend, do not renew my sorrows by making me tell the reason for this dog's weeping, for in so doing my heart would be so grieved that before I could come to the end of my story, my life would be over." The chaste woman begged more insistently, and the wicked old woman began her narration in the following tearful and grievous manner: "This dog here weeping was my own daughter who, in other times, was a very beautiful and chaste woman. She was loved and courted by a young man, more than one can say. The young man, without hope because she set great value on her continence, fell into an incurable sickness caused by the grief and affliction that came from his love affair. For this reason, the gods took pity on this young man, and to punish my daughter for not consenting to his pleas, they turned her into a little dog, as you can see. And so acceptably did the young man pray and beg, weeping before the gods, that they granted his request and supplication." And so the old lady related the case, showing in the telling such great woe and sadness that she could hardly finish her story.

To this the honest woman replied: "Oh well beloved, you have frightened me and perturbed my heart so that I do not know what to say, because I myself have committed another such crime. A young man seeks me so frequently with such love and affection that it appears as if he wished to die for my love, but because of my chastity and the affection in which I hold my husband, I have scorned all his advances." The old lady said: "Beloved friend, I advise you to listen to his pleas as rapidly as you can, so that you may prevent another case like the one in which my daughter was turned into a little dog."

The woman said: "I shall no longer reject this man so that I do not oppose the gods. If this man loves me, I shall not deny him the office of love. And if he does not ask me, I shall offer myself if I can find him." And with this, the old lady thanked the chaste woman and went home. The old woman took the young man news that agreed with his desire, and so she joined the lover with the beloved and won the thanks of both of them.

Fable 12. Of the Blind Man and the Adulterous Adolescent

There was once a blind man who had a very beautiful wife, and he guarded her chastity with great diligence because he was very jealous. One day they were both in a garden in the shade of a pear tree, and with his consent, she climbed up to pick the pears. The blind man, who was very suspicious lest someone else climb up into the tree after her, embraced the trunk while his wife was up in the tree. But as the fruit tree had many branches, there was a youth hidden there who had climbed up beforehand to wait for the wife of the blind man. The young man joined her joyfully, and the two began to play the game of Venus.

The blind man heard the sounds of this, and he began to cry out in sorrow: "O wicked wife, although I lack sight, I do not for that reason fail to hear and feel; rather, my other senses are more intense, and I believe that you have there with you some adulterer. I complain of this to our sovereign god Jupiter, who can mend with joy the hearts of the sad and can restore sight to the blind." These words spoken, the vision of the blind man was restored and he was given his natural sight. Looking up, he saw the adulterous young man with his wife, and he called out suddenly: "O most deceitful and falsest of wives, why do you play these tricks upon me when I believed you to be chaste and good? Woe is me, for I do not henceforth expect to have any happiness with you."

She, hearing her husband scold her, was at first frightened, but with happy countenance and a new-found malice, she answered her husband in a clear sounding voice: "I give thanks to all the gods that they have heard my prayers and have restored my beloved husband's sight. My beloved lord, know that the sight that you received is given by my prayers and good works. Up to now I have done in vain much that the doctors have recommended. Finally I begged again and made pleas and prayers to the gods for your sight. The god Mercury, by command of the sovereign Jupiter, appeared to me in my dreams and told me that I should climb a tree called the pear where I should play the game of Venus with a young man, and thus your sight would be restored to you. This I have done for your welfare and health, and you should give thanks to the gods and especially to me since it was through me that you have won your sight."

The blind man, believing the deceitful words of his wife, was reconciled to her and received her as a good woman, thinking that his reproach was undeserved. He gave many thanks and rewarded her with many gifts for her outstanding service.

Fable 13. Of the Cleverness and Astuteness of a Wife against Her Husband, a Winegrower

A deceitful woman very quickly invents fraudulent excuses with which to cover her misdeeds, as this fable shows. A rustic went to care for his vineyard, so his wife, thinking that he would be a long time in returning, as was usually the case, sent for her lover. They were having intercourse and taking great pleasure in their illicit will, satisfying their desire and appetite, when the husband suddenly knocked at the door, arriving with an eye injured by a branch. The wife, overcome with fear, hid her lover in a bedroom and then opened the door for her husband. Entering the house in anguish and with great pain in his eye, he ordered his wife to prepare the bed in that room so that he might rest. But she, fearing that on entering the room he would see her lover within, said to her husband: "Why do you insist so violently on throwing yourself upon that bed? Tell me first what misfortune has befallen you."

The husband told her all about the cause of his ill fortune, and she said: "Permit me, my beloved lord, to cure your uninjured eye in a way I know so that the other eye which is damaged and hurt may not trouble you, as often happens, and so that my eyes may not be damaged in the same fashion. Damage to my eyes would trouble you no less than damage to your own, for between you and me all things are in common."

In this way, pretending and giving to understand that she was healing him with her mouth, she covered the good eye, warming and comforting it with her breath until her lover came out of the room and safely went away without the husband realizing it. When her lover was safe, the wife said: "From now on, my good husband, you will be safe from the damage that can come to your good eye from the injured one, and so, when you like you may go into the bedroom." And with this quickly invented and fraudulent trick, the woman deceived her husband and sent her lover away without danger.

Fable 14. Of the Merchant's Wife and Her Old Mother-in-Law

This fable tells of a very deceitful old lady who did not wish her daughter to keep her chastity. A merchant who went from country to country on business left his wife in the care of his mother-in-law. As the wife was very young, she fell in love with a young man and told her secret to her mother, who, abetting her daughter in her illicit amours, sent for the young man. Knowing that the mother consented to his proposal and desire and taking great pleasure in it, the young man went to them and was received joyfully in their dwelling. All three of them began to eat and drink with gusto, thinking to carry out his wishes as he desired.

While they were eating, the husband came knocking at the door. The woman, rather frightened and hiding the friend, went to open the door. As he entered, the husband ordered them to make ready the bed as he wished to rest because he was tired. The wife was frightened by this, knowing that the lover was hidden near the bed. She did not know what to do, and the mother, seeing her daughter stutter and hesitate, said to her: "Daughter, stop making the bed so that we can show your husband, my beloved son, the sheet that we made." Then the old lady took down the cover from the clothes rack and, holding up one end of it, ordered her daughter to hold up the other end, thus placing the sheet between the husband and themselves and allowing the young man to leave without the merchant's suspecting the deceit. So the old lady said: "Now you may put the sheet on the bed for it is very clean, woven and sewn with our hands." The husband, being grateful, said: "Blessed are you who are so clever and learned in this skill." And they said: "We are able to do other things even better than this; if you want to see them now we shall be happy to show them." And, deceived in this manner, the merchant lay down to rest in his bed.

Fable 15. By Poggio. About the Wife and the Husband Shut Up in the Dove Cote

The astuteness and sharpness of women makes the timorous bold, as is proven in this fable. A man named Pedro had an adulterous compact with the wife of an ignorant farmer, and all three of them were related to one another. This farmer, fearing the lawmen who pursued him because of a certain debt, often slept in the fields. Once when Pedro went in to the farmer's wife, as he had many times before, the husband came home. Seeing this, the wife placed her lover beneath the bed and began to upbraid her husband, saying that he deserved to be caught and placed in jail because just then the lawmen were looking in every house in order to capture him. They even said they would keep coming until they had found him. Hearing these words, the farmer became frightened and looked for a way to leave the house for the fields, but as the gates of the town were shut, he gave it up. His wife said: "Oh unlucky man, what are you doing? If they catch you, it is certain you will never get out of jail."

The unhappy farmer asked his wife's advice, and she, ready for deceit, said: "Climb into the dove cote where you will be safe tonight, for I shall lock the door and take away the ladder so that they may not suspect that you are there." The man did as his wife advised, and shut himself in the dove cote, which was locked on the outside so that he could not get out unless his wife opened it for him. Having done this, she got her lover out from under the bed. He pretended to be a deputy and constable and began to speak with great vigor and in a loud voice to the wife, asking for her husband and looking for him all over the house so that the poor husband who was hidden was very frightened. When the excitement, commotion, and shouting ceased, the wife and her lover both went to bed calmly as they had wanted to do. And so the good man was deceived by his wife, being content to sleep in the droppings of the doves since he thus escaped from justice.

Fable 16. Of the Woman Who Gave Birth to a Child by the Grace of God, Her Husband Being Absent

Those who live in the city of Gayeta seek their living by sailing the seas. A poor shipmaster who lived near Gayeta left his young wife at home and went to seek a living in other places, and so was a long time away. After five years he came back to his house to visit his wife who, since her husband had been so long away, feared that he would not return and had accommodated herself with another man. Returning home, the husband found her better clothed than when he had left her, and he marveled, since he had left his wife with little cash. Before, the house had been in bad repair, but she had restored it, adorned it, and decorated it. The wife said: "Sir, do not be astonished at this, for the grace of God has helped me, as He has given great gifts to many people." The husband said: "Thanks be to God who has helped us thus." Seeing also the bedroom and the bed more ornate and all the paraphernalia of the house very clean and in order, he asked his wife where she had acquired such property. She said that with the kindness and grace of God it had been given to her. So at length the husband gave great praise to God for having been so liberal with them, and he praised the magnificence of God no less for all the other improvements that he found in the house.

Finally there appeared in the house a bonny and graceful baby more than three years old who caressed his mother. Seeing the child, the husband asked whose it was, and the woman replied, "It is mine." He, marveling at this, said: "And where did this child come from in my absence?" The woman affirmed boldly that the very grace and mercy of God had given him to her. Then the master of the ship said with great anger: "Since the grace of God knows how to procreate children in my wife, for that grace I thank him but little, because it seems to me that he intervenes too much in my affairs. It was enough that he should help me in other matters, but creating children in my wife during my absence, that is nothing to be grateful for."

Fable 17. Of the Devil and the Wicked Old Woman

Let him who desires to end his days in good and certain peace keep away from the company and conversation of wicked and false old women, for under heaven scarcely was anything made that is more vile and deceitful than such old women. But God forbid that it should be understood that in this fable I mean to criticize the condition of honest and chaste women, who are worthy of all honor and reverence. Rather, this fable is written in this way in praise of these women so that they may keep themselves away from such diabolical old women and that they may not be caught up in evil and deceived by them and by their conversation.

A man distinguished for his good life and honest ways took for a wife a woman with whom he lived for many years in peace and love. There was never any difference between them, and their concord was of such an extent

that all the neighbors wondered at their honest companionship. The devil, who knows an infinite number of tricks and is the enemy of all good works, saw this good fellowship of husband and wife and grieved more than one can say. Night and day sowing discord, he insisted with all his might that the love and unity that bound them together could be perverted and destroyed.

For a long time both he and his minions tried to turn that concord into discord, but they did not succeed. Now, losing all hope, the devil explained the matter to an old bearded woman, asking her to help him in some ways. She said: "With my talents, this is an easy thing that I may accomplish very quickly. For a small reward I will do what will please you, for I will place between them such deeds and discords as until today were never placed between man and wife so that there will be more dissonance between them than there ever was affection." The devil said: "What do you want from me for this work?" She said: "Certainly this will require but little effort on my part. Therefore I only ask you to give me a pair of shoes." To this the devil replied: "Not a single pair but enough shoes to last you for a year will I give you."

Then the old lady went to the good woman, and after she had talked about a number of things, she said to her: "I certainly spent as painful and unpleasant a night as you could imagine." The honest woman asked what made her endure such tribulation, and the old lady answered: "I beg you not to say anything to your husband about what I wish to tell you, or show yourself disturbed, but receive him cheerfully. The cause of my tribulation is this: he has a young girl whose name I keep silent for decency's sake and for her reputation. She is visited by him each day, and this is a very secret affair, and if I did not fear that he might kill you in order not to be bothered, I would not have told you about it. However, if you want my advice, I will tell you a way that will make him love no one but yourself."

Much disturbed in her heart and mind, the good woman spoke as follows: "Up to now, no manner of evil or of dishonor have I found in my husband, but if the things you say are true, you may be able to help me, anguished as I am in this matter. From now on, I am yours and will do everything you may ask of me." The old lady then said: "Your husband has a hair on his throat, and if you should cut it off while he is sleeping, he will not be able to love another save yourself." The good woman, believing this, agreed to follow the woman's advice.

After receiving many thanks, the old lady departed and went quickly to where the husband was toiling. Among many other things, she said these words to him: "Oh man of good condition and breeding, I have compassion and mercy on you, for your wife, who is of good and honored stock and whom you love as yourself, not only loves another but has decided to kill you in order to run away with him. I know that it is agreed between them that she will cut your throat with a razor. If by chance you do not believe me, pretend to sleep during the day and you will see through experience that I am speaking the truth. Take care to avoid sleeping and you will be able to avenge yourself at your pleasure." The husband, terrified by this horrible news, groaned and said: "Certainly up till now I have never seen any fault or anything irregular about my wife, nor has anyone ever said such things. But if what you say is true, I have much to thank you for. I shall use your advice."

The man went back to his house, and after he had eaten, he acted tired and let his head fall over the chair, and according to the old woman's advice, he acted as if he were sleeping deeply. The good woman, believing he was asleep, took the razor that she had ready and tried to cut the hair from his throat. The husband, believing she wished to cut his throat, took the razor by force and with it killed his wife.

After the old woman had done this awful deed by trickery and cleverness, she said to the devil: "Give me the shoes you promised me; it looks as if I have deserved them." He answered: "You deserve much more than the shoes, for you outdo us all in malice, deceit, and cleverness, but I do not think it is right for you to come closer to me than you are now or to touch or feel me with your hands." Then the devil, for fear that she might deceive him or poison him with her malice, gave the old woman a stick with all the shoes tied at the end. Keeping a barrier between the old woman and himself, he gave them to her and said: "O pestiferous and vile lady, receive your profit and thanks. Go away from here in any direction you choose, for the farther removed you are from us the better we will love you. Although we are wicked, petty, and abhorred by everyone, even so we do not wish to receive you into our company because you are full of deceit and wickedness and could not do anything but evil to us."

So perished that honorable man and his wife through the false counsel of the old woman. Therefore, everyone should avoid old women and not believe their words even lightly, for they are more inclined to evil than to good. Rather we should believe those whose fame, trustworthiness, and works have been tried and proven.

Fable 18. Of the Master Tailor, the King, and His Servants

To pay back a deceit and return another for it is a common practice. Do not do to another what you do not wish to have done to you, this fable tells. A king had a good master tailor who knew well how to cut clothing and vestments for any sort of weather and for suitable persons of all kinds. The tailor had many apprentices, one of whom was named Nedio, who excelled among the rest in skill at sewing.

As a feast day was approaching, the king called the tailor and ordered him to make some fancy clothes for him and his entourage. In order that the tailor might do this most expeditiously, the king ordered a chamberlain named Eumicus to provide all the things necessary for the maestro and his disciples, ordering him also to supply them abundantly with food.

One day the chamberlain had them given warm bread with honey, telling them to save some honey for Nedio, who was absent. And the maestro said: "Nedio does not eat honey." So they ate it all up, but after they had eaten, Nedio arrived and asked: "Why did you eat without me? It seems that you did not keep my share for me." The chamberlain answered: "Your master told me that you do not eat honey, so for that reason we did not save any for you." Nedio was silent, thinking how he might play a similar joke on his master.

One day, the master being absent, the chamberlain asked Nedio if he had ever seen a better stitcher than his master. He replied: "The master would be a very good stitcher if his unfortunate illness did not interfere with him and torment him." The chamberlain asked what malady that was, and Nedio replied: "My master is mad to such a point that when it seizes him, he would kill or maim everyone present." The chamberlain said: "If I knew when his mania would seize him, I would tie him up so that he might do no harm." The disciple said: "When you see him look at the table, this way and that, striking the table with his hands, and when he gets up from his seat and takes from it what he finds there, you can tell that his madness is upon him. If you are not careful, he is no less likely to strike you than us." Eumicus relied: "Blessed are you for warning me! I shall save myself and the rest of you from him."

The following day Nedio secretly hid his master's scissors. Looking for them but not finding them, the master began to strike the table and look this way and that, and he got up from his chair striking out with his hands. When the chamberlain saw this, he ordered his servants to tie up the master so that he might not strike anyone, and he had him whipped as a punishment. The master, feeling the harm they did him but not knowing the cause, complained in a loud voice, asking why they were striking him without reason. They did not cease to beat him because they thought he was mad and they wanted to bring him back to his senses. After they grew tired of hitting him they untied him, and with long groans and complaints, he began to ask the chamberlain why he had been so cruelly beaten. The chamberlain replied that he had had it done for his benefit because his disciple Nedio had told them that sometimes the master went mad and his frenzy seized him. Nedio said that if they did not tie him up and punish him, the master would not cease to do evil and to strike those present, and he would not recover from that illness unless he was tied and whipped; this Nedio ordered done to cure the master.

The master said to the disciple: "O cruel and malicious man, when did you ever see me mad?" The disciple replied: "I saw you go mad when you believed that I did not eat honey." The chamberlain and all present heard these things, laughed loudly and judged that the master had suffered sufficient misfortune. He who plays a joke on another may expect to be made fun of and deceived, and he who does not wish to be deceived should not do to another what he would not like to have done to himself.

Fable 19. Of the Madman and the Gentleman Hunter

That one should discontinue a trade in which the costs exceed the profits, this story proves. In the city of Milan there was once a famous physician whose duty it was to cure any sort of madness or mental disorder. He had this way of curing the mad: he had in his house an enclosure in which there was a pool of very viscous and stinking water. Here he tied each madman to a pillar; he took off each man's clothes and put him in mud up to his knees or even deeper according to the nature and quality of his madness. The physician made them stay there on a regimen of treatment until he felt they were cured.

They tell me that he was brought one madman among many others, whom he put in that pond up to his thighs. Having been there two weeks, the madman returned to his senses, and he asked the physician to take him out of there because he was quite sane. The physician took him out of the water and his torment, but he forbade him to leave the enclosure. The man was obedient for some days and did as the doctor commanded, and the physician had pity on him and let him leave. He ordered him to go about inside the house but not to go out of the door. The madman, thus cured, walked joyfully all over the house keeping well the command of his master.

Once at the door, the madman saw a man coming on horseback with a falcon and two or three greyhounds and bird dogs. The madman called out to him, as he was moved by the novelty of what he saw because he did not remember that he had ever seen them before. The horseman came up to him, and the madman asked: "Who are you? Listen to me a moment if you please. Tell me, that thing on which you came, what is it, and why do you have it?" The man answered: "That is a horse, and I have it in order to hunt." The madman also asked: "What do you have in your hand?" The horseman answered: "That is a falcon, and it is useful for hunting partridges and cranes." The madman also asked about the dogs, and the man told him they too were useful for the hunt since they find hares, rabbits, birds, and other game. The madman then asked: "What would be the value of your game in a year?" The horseman answered: "I could not tell you exactly, but I think that it would not be worth less than four pounds of gold." The madman asked: "How much do you spend on your horse, falcons, and dogs in a year?" And he on horseback replied: "I may spend more than fifty pounds as a rule."

Marveling at the madness of the horseman, the madman said: "I beg you to go from here quickly, flying if you can, so that the physician may not see you. If he finds you here and learns of your great madness, he will put you into a pond of water with the other madmen, and to my way of thinking deeper than the other because your madness is greater." This fable shows that the hunting and other practices in which the expense is greater than the gain are to be discontinued if a man wishes to be reputed wise, discreet, and sound of mind.

Fable 20. Of the Priest, His Dog, and the Bishop

Generous gifts and services may atone for many transgressions, even the violation of a sacred place, as this fable shows. In Tuscany there was an ignorant but very rich priest. He buried in a cemetery a much beloved dog of his. The bishop noticed the priest's excess; he knew that the cleric was rich, which aggravated his offense, and he had the cleric called before himself for punishment. The priest knew that the bishop would accept a gift of money rather than punish him physically. As satisfactory repentance he took with him certain pieces of gold and went before the bishop.

The cleric was reprehended for the burial of the dog, and the bishop ordered him taken to jail to be punished. The priest, seeing himself in these straits, said to the bishop: "O father, if you but knew the wisdom of that dog you would not marvel that I had it buried among men; he certainly exceeded in sharpness all the genius of man in life as in death." The bishop wondered at this and asked: "What is it you say?" The priest replied: "At his death the dog made a will, and considering to what extent you were in need of money for the great expenses that you incur for the church of God, he left one hundred pieces of gold for your work, which I now give you." The bishop, approving of the will and the burial, ordered the gold to be kept for necessary affairs, and he released the priest in question from his crime. This clearly signifies that money may win a pardon even for very grave faults.

Fable 21. Of the Ape and the Nuts

A great reward is often earned by hard and continuous work. If a man is not discouraged from a task by the seriousness and labor that are necessary to do it, he may complete it in the end, as this fable informs us. An ape standing beneath a walnut tree asked the name of the tree and the value of its fruit. He was told that that nut tree produced very tasty kernels, and he began to enjoy himself, thinking that he could use those nuts as he desired. The tree was great and tall and without branches until half way up, and the ape could not get his arms around the tree nor jump up into it. He went to a house near the walnut grove where he asked a man to lend him a ladder so that he might climb up the tree and eat the nuts. He dragged the ladder to the tree with great difficulty and arranged it there in such a way that he was able to go aloft. Joyfully he climbed up, took a nut, and bit into it through its green shell. He tasted the bitterness of the shell and threw the nut away in disgust. He tried another three or four, but finding them rather bitter and not any better in taste than the first one, he tossed them away with great distaste without trying to find the meat within.

Then, full of woe and after many sighs, he said: "Cursed be they who showed me these nuts, praised them, and then gave me help and advised me to eat them. In all the days of my life I have never striven so nor taken such pains, but I have accomplished nothing save to waste my time because the sweetness of the fruit has turned into bitterness." Having said these words, he went away groaning and sighing. This means that no one should discontinue a project begun, however difficult it is; instead, one ought to think of the end result which is a reward for the effort. If one diligently undertakes a task he will overcome his grief, for as the proverb says: *Dulcia non meruir qui amara non gustavit.* That is: "He does not deserve the sweet who does not like the bitter."

Fable 22. Of the Father and Son Who Went to Sell an Ass

He who wishes to please everybody and follow their advice cannot long escape scorn nor maintain his estate, as this story tells. A father and son went to sell an ass at a fair, and they kept the ass in front of them with no load. They met a great company of men who were talking about them as follows: "Oh, how silly and ignorant these men are. They feed the ass, but they do not profit from him. They could ride upon him, and thus they would exercise his muscles and would stop wearing out their shoes. The ass would feel no pain as he appears to be strong and resilient, especially since the only reason for his being is to do work." The father heard these words, and so he had the son ride on the ass while he went on foot.

They were going in this manner when they met others coming from the city who came up to them and said: "What obvious folly is this? This man is

fairly old and because of weakness can barely move his feet, but instead of riding the donkey himself, he puts the son, who could come running after him like a buck, on the donkey. This is bad rearing and custom and could cause the boy to become lazy and unambitious." The good old man knew that this was correct advice, so he had his son get off and he mounted the ass himself. They started off again, the son following on foot. They were finally observed by other travelers who, like the previous ones, began to criticize the man: "Oh, cruel and hardhearted is this father to his son; he has more pity on the ass than on his son whom he makes work too hard by going on foot in this heat. It may be that the son will weaken his body and limbs and become injured and lame so that in his old age he may frequent the hospital." The father, feeling the effect of these words, then had his son ride behind him on the ass, and so the ass went on loaded with both of them.

Riding thus they encountered other travelers who were even more critical than the others: "Look, two men on one donkey. We might even say that there are two asses riding an ass. The poor creature can scarcely stand on his feet, tired as he is, but they pay no attention to this. Certainly it would be better to carry the donkey if they did not wish to soon see him dead." The father, thinking about the men's advice, said to his son: "It seems to me that these men have reasoned well. So that the donkey may not die but may recover, let us tie his feet together with a rope, put a stick in between them, and carry him to the city. We can do this without much difficulty, and we will gain public goodwill for being kind men even to dumb animals. The donkey will rest and we will sell him and receive a profit from our action."

Carrying the ass with his feet tied, they now came upon many travelers who made fun of them, saying: "Who ever saw an ass have such wit that he ordered these other beasts to carry him, even though he is capable of bearing them both with his strength. They carry him and feed him when he was made for no other purpose than to serve men. Since they do not make use of him as they ought to, it would be better that they should flay him, leave his carcass, and profit by his hide rather than going loaded with him suffering so much shame and everyone laughing at them." The father, hearing all this, was moved by great anger and took the stick with which they carried the ass and gave him a great blow on the head so that he fell dead upon the ground. The man began to skin him, saying: "Oh, how many insults have we borne today on account of this donkey! Now I think our dishonor will be at an end."

Finishing the skinning, he took the hide, threw it over his shoulder, and carried it into the city. In the city he went to the market where he might sell the skin and use the money to help pay his expenses. Some boys, seeing how bloody and wet was the ass's skin which the old man had, followed the ill-breeding and custom of always doing more harm than good and began to grab at the skin, first on one side and then on the other. They dragged it through the mud and dirtied the old man's face so that he looked like a scarecrow. So, this good man escaped half dead and with damaged belongings because he wanted to please everyone.

This parable teaches us that there is no man in the world, great or small, of whatever condition, whose acts are not criticized and murmured against. What some praise in him, others will criticize, but he should not leave off following reason to try to please everyone. One ought to consider whether the criticism is just or unjust; if it is just, receive it and reform one's life, but if the criticism is frivolous and unjust, pay no attention to it since we are all different in our inclinations. To one person a certain thing seems good and proper, but the same thing displeases others since we cannot all like the same thing.

Therefore, I do not expect to escape criticism in my translation of this book into the Spanish language, because the work is not so much elegant as pleasant for the common and uneducated folk for whose solace and teaching was intended. We are all prone to criticize the deeds of others and desirous of hearing our own praise rather than enduring the defensible praise which is not ours. I beg the prudent and the literate to listen to my treatise with benevolent intent, and I hope they are more inclined toward defense than criticism. Let the reader, the judge of judges without witnesses, assess the cases with kindness and pity.

Here ends the illustrated *Book of Aesop,* the fables brought together with the principle of advantageous morality and applied to the correction and improvement of human behavior. Collected here are

the fables of Remitius, Avianus, Doligamus, Alfonso, and Poggio
with others of an extraneous sort which were translated from Latin
into Romance and published in the very noble and loyal city
of Saragossa by Johann Hurus, by birth a German from Costantia,
in the year of our Lord 1489.

Bibliography

Baldwin, Spurgeon W. "The Role of the Moral in *La vida del Ysopet con sus fabulas hystoriadas.*" *Hispania* 47 (1954): 762-65.

Beardsley, Theodore S. *Hispanic-Classical Translations Printed between 1482 and 1699.* Pittsburgh: Duquesne Univ. Press, 1970.

Bédier, Joseph. *Les Fabliaux: Etude de littérature populaire et d'histoire littéraire du moyen âge.* Paris: Bouillon, 1885.

Burrus, Victoria, and Harriet Goldberg. *Esopete ystoriado (Toulouse, 1488): Edition, Study and Notes.* Madison: Hispanic Seminary of Medieval Studies, 1990.

Deyermond, Alan. *The Literary History of Spain: The Middle Ages.* New York: Barnes and Noble, 1971.

Dunlop, Alan John. *History of Fiction.* London: Bell, 1889.

Fábulas de Esopo, reproducción en facsímile de la Primera Edición de 1489. Madrid: Real Academia Española, 1929.

González Palencia, Angel. *Historia de la literatura arábigo-española.* 2d ed. Barcelona: Editorial Labor, 1945.

Hervieux, Léopold. *Les Fabulistes latins. IV. Etudes de Cheriton et ses dérivés.* Paris: Librairie de Fermin-Didot, 1896.

Hirschman, Joan. *Aesop's Fables.* New York: Dell, 1964.

Jacobs, Joseph. *History of the Aesopic Fable.* London: Nutt, 1889.

Keller, John E. *Motif Index of Mediaeval Spanish Exempla.* Knoxville: Univ. of Tennessee Press, 1949.

―――. *El libro de los gatos. Edición Crítica.* Madrid-Valencia: Consejo Superior de Investigaciones Científicas, 1958.

―――. *El libro de los engaños.* Revised Spanish Edition. Textos Antiguos Españoles, no. 1. Valencia: Artes Gráficas Soler, 1959.

―――. *El libro de los engaños e asayamientos de las mugeres.* Studies in the Romance Languages and Literatures no. 20, 2d ed. Chapel Hill: Univ. of North Carolina Press, 1959.

―――. *Libro de los exenplos por a.b.c. Edición Crítica.* Madrid: Consejo Superior de Investigaciones Científicas, 1961.

―――. *El libro de Calila e Digna. Edición Crítica.* Madrid: Consejo Superior de Investigaciones Científicas, 1965

―――. *Barlaam e Josafat. Edición Crítica.* Madrid: Consejo Superior de Investigaciones Científicas, 1980.

————, and James H. Johnson. "Motif-Index Classification of the Fables and Tales of *Ysopete Hystoriado*." *Southern Folklore Quarterly* 18 (1954): 85-117.

————, with Joseph R. Jones. *The Scholar's Guide*. Translation of the *Disciplina Clericalis* of Pedro Alfonso. Toronto: Pontifical Institute of Mediaeval Studies, 1969.

————, and Richard P. Kinkade. *Iconography in Medieval Spanish Literature*. Lexington: Univ. Press of Kentucky, 1984.

Lenaghan, R.T., ed. *Caxton's Aesop*. Cambridge: Harvard Univ. Press, 1967.

McKendry, J.M. *Aesop: Five Centuries of Illustrated Fables*. New York: Metropolitan Museum, 1935.

Menéndez y Pelayo, Marcelino. *Orígenes de la novela*. Santander: Consejo Superior de Investigaciones Científicas, 1948.

Millares Carlo, A. *Historia de la literatura española hasta fines del siglo XV*. México: Clásicos y Modernos, 5, 1950.

Navarro, Carmen. "El incunable de 1482 y las ediciones del *Isopete* en España." *Quaderni di Lingue e Letterature* 15 (1990): 157-64.

Perry, Ben. *Aesopica: Greek and Latin Texts*. Vol. 1. Urbana: Univ. of Illinois Press, 1952.

Swan, Charles. *The Tales of the "Gesta Romanorum" Translated from Latin*. Revised by Wynnard Hooper. New York: Everest Books, 1958.

Welter, J.P. *L'exemplum dans la littérature religieuse et didactique du Moyen Age*. Paris: Occitania, 1914.

Wright, Thomas. *A Selection of Latin Stories from Manuscripts of the 13th and 14th Centuries*. Percy Society Publications, vol. 8. London: Richards, 1843.

Index